George Phillips Bev

British Manufacturing Industries

George Phillips Bevan

British Manufacturing Industries

ISBN/EAN: 9783743309937

Manufactured in Europe, USA, Canada, Australia, Japa

Cover: Foto ©ninafisch / pixelio.de

Manufactured and distributed by brebook publishing software (www.brebook.com)

George Phillips Bevan

British Manufacturing Industries

BRITISH MANUFACTURING INDUSTRIES.

EDITED BY

G. PHILLIPS BEVAN, F.G.S.

JEWELLERY,
By George Wallis (South Kensington Museum).

GOLD WORKING,
By Rev. Charles Boutell, M.A.

WATCHES AND CLOCKS,
By F. J. Britten (British Horological Institute).

MUSICAL INSTRUMENTS,
By E. F. Rimbault, LL.D. (Musical Examiner, College of Preceptors).

CUTLERY,
By F. Callis (Sheffield).

LONDON:
EDWARD STANFORD, 55, CHARING CROSS.

1876.

PREFACE.

The object of this series is to bring into one focus the leading features and present position of the most important industries of the kingdom, so as to enable the general reader to comprehend the enormous development that has taken place within the last twenty or thirty years. It is evident that the great increase in education throughout the country has tended largely to foster a simultaneous interest in technical knowledge, as evinced by the spread of Art and Science Schools, Trade Museums, International Exhibitions, &c.; and this fact is borne out by a perusal of the daily papers, in which the prominence given to every improvement in trade or machinery attests the desire of the reading public to know more about these matters. Here, however, the difficulty commences, for the only means of acquiring this information are from handbooks to the various manufactures (which are usually too minute in detail for general instruction), from trade journals and the reports of scientific societies; and to obtain and systematize these scattered details is a labour and a tax upon time and patience which comparatively few persons care to surmount. In these volumes all these facts are gathered together and presented in as readable a form as is compatible with accuracy and a freedom from superficiality; and though they do not lay claim to being a technical guide to each industry, the names of the contributors are a sufficient guarantee that they are a reliable and standard work of reference. Great stress is laid on the progressive developments of the manufactures, and the various applications to them of the collateral arts and sciences; the history of each is truly given, while present processes and recent inventions are succinctly described.

BRITISH MANUFACTURING INDUSTRIES.

JEWELLERY.

By George Wallis (South Kensington Museum).

The love of personal decoration is inherent in man, and is characteristic alike of the condition of savage and civilized life. We have no record of a people, however primitive, in whom the desire for ornament of some kind has not existed, and did not manifest itself in some tangible and unmistakable form, either by tattooing devices on the body itself, or suspending to the ears, nose, and lips, metal or other ornaments, either by perforation of the cartilage or by pressure. The decoration of the head, by a bandage across the forehead; of the neck, by a collar; of the arms and wrists, the legs and ankles, and finally the fingers and toes, appears to grow by a systematic order of procession from the minutest ornament, up to the most redundant and elaborate display of the jeweller's art, as seen amongst the wealthiest orientalists of past and present times. Nor would it be very difficult to trace in the intricate tattooings or "cast" marks of semi-savage peoples, the basis of design on which the general forms, and especially the minuter details of the jewellery of a later condition of social and domestic life have been grounded. The use too of suitable natural objects, such as shells, seed vessels, seeds, feathers, drilled stones—either singly or in repetition and combination, has been largely suggestive of an important class of personal decorations produced in metal, especially amongst the people of the East.

It would probably be too much to say that the more primitive peoples had always some representative purpose in what they wore in the way of personal adornment; but that they appear to have had an instructive appreciation of the fitness of what they wore for the purpose for which they wore it, may be safely asserted: indeed just as much as the tattooed badges of the chieftain recorded his deeds and marked his rank in his tribe, or "nation," or the decorations of civilized society mark the conventional position, or the actual public services of the wearer.

In thus indicating a common origin, however remote, for much of the personal ornament used and worn under varying conditions by every people in the world, it is not by any means intended to set aside the fact, that the application of decorative design, in form and detail, to the instruments necessary for fastening clothing upon the person of the wearer, has not largely influenced the nature of the materials selected, the character of the contrivance, and the outward form and appearance of innumerable objects in use from the earliest periods, down to the present time; and to which the generic name of jewellery is now given.

A jewel is not necessarily an object of use, but it must be one of precious material, or materials fitted for use as a personal ornament. The word is said to come to us through the French from the Latin *gaudium* (joy);—*jouel*, *joyau*; and though it is sometimes used to describe a single precious stone, it is not in this sense that I intend to use it, but in its wider and more general signification.

As in many other matters connected with the industrial arts, we turn to ancient Egypt for the earliest illustrations of working in gold, and the use of vitreous substances for giving variety of colour in combination with fitness of form to use, and to enhance the expression of the symbol which invariably suggests the basis of the design. The Egyptian mode of sepulture has been the means by which admirable examples of the jeweller's art, as practised long prior to the existence of such an industry amongst any other people of which we have record, have come down to us. The fact that the most cherished and valuable personal ornaments of the dead were buried with them in sarcophagi, lavishly decorated, preserved these valuable illustrations of the manners and skill of a people long since passed away, as shown in the International Exhibitions of 1862 and 1867, by the remarkable collection of Egyptian jewellery belonging to the Khedive of Egypt. These were discovered by M. Mariette near Thebes, and were taken from the coffin of Queen Aah

Hoteb, found at the entrance to the Valley of the Tomb of the Kings.

As might be expected, this jewellery partook in its design and execution of all the leading characteristics of the arts of a people, which had left such extraordinary monuments of greatness and power behind them. They showed unmistakably that the artificers who produced them were well acquainted with the various handicrafts of hammered work, chasing, and soldering; that they had full knowledge of and mastery over the processes by which inlays of coloured materials were used as an adjunct to the gold, or in which the gold itself was subordinated and simply used as a vehicle for displaying colour, and that, like all the Oriental peoples of later times, they had used the means at their disposal to imitate or suggest the effect of the combination of precious stones, which, if abundant, were not so well adapted to the special purpose they had in view, since their artistic imitation in vitreous substances was more under command for the purposes of surface decoration. We shall see in due course how this system was carried out in later times and with what extraordinary results.

The only record of any value of the use of jewels, or jewellery, by the Assyrians, is found in the bas-reliefs of this ancient people. Their use of personal ornament is here shown in a very distinct manner, but we can know nothing of the character of the workmanship.

Discussing the question as to whether the Phœnicians were manufacturers as well as merchants, since specimens attributed to them have been considered as more likely to have been early Asiatic Greek, the gold trinkets and jewellery of the Etruscans present the first practical lesson after the Egyptian. The specimens of the handicraft power of Etruscan goldsmiths and jewellers, which have come down to us, show a skill in these arts some six or seven hundred years before the Christian era which are not surpassed, and in some respects cannot be equalled, by any modern workers in gold; and our method of decorating, or giving tone and richness to the surface of the metal by granulation of that surface, has only recently been attempted to be imitated with a certain measure of success. Signor A. Castillani, of Rome, has attempted to revive the old Etruscan methods, and in this he has been assisted by the tenacity of tradition amongst the workmen living in the Abruzzi, and by bringing their skill and methods, handed down from generation to generation, to bear upon modern wants. Castillani's examples of this class of jewellery in its recent revival by him, exhibited at the International Exhibition of 1872, were remarkable specimens of past methods, successfully applied to meet modern wants and ideas in the most refined and elegant form.

As might be expected, the Greeks left their impress upon an art in which refinement in design and skill in handicraft power has so much to do with success; but then it was with them, as it unhappily is *not* with us, that the designer and the workman were united in one person. Thus the thought and its realization were one. The Greeks excelled, as might be expected, in the character of the models selected, in the finish which they brought to bear upon the work by chasing, in the remarkable manner in which they united by soldering the thinnest pieces of metal, as also in their intaglio work; whilst they also used the granulated surfaces already spoken of in connection with Etruscan work, and with equal success. The freedom with which the Greeks treated the forms they adopted in their objects of personal decoration is remarkable, and in this they simply took skilful advantage of the thinness of the metal, to avoid the most rigid treatment required in greater masses of material.

Roman jewellery, like Roman art generally, is little more than a reflex of Greek. In short there can be little doubt that it was for the most part the production of Greeks, working in a less refined spirit. The Roman conquered, or purchased, the means of luxury and refinement, and the Greek was ready to administer to both. At a late period Egyptian and Asiatic forms find their way into Roman jewellery. Rings were largely used upon the fingers, a fashion said to have been derived from the Etruscans, and from the size and character of some of these which have come down to modern times, they were probably marks of official authority. There are, amongst the rings acquired in the Waterton Collection, now in the South Kensington Museum, some of the time of Pliny, which are decorated with open work, being pierced through at the sides of the bezel and the shoulder, whilst occasionally the whole ring is perforated.

The next distinct style of manufacture, passing over

the Byzantine period as one of transition, is that known as the Merovingian of the fifth century, and the Anglo-Saxon of later date. With them may be associated the Celtic, all finally leading to the mediæval jewellery popularly known as the Gothic. We have orientalism running through all these, of a character more or less marked, but ever modified by the peculiar spirit of each age, yet ever preserving the traditions of the goldsmiths' art in the application of details, and the adaptation of forms to use.

The Merovingian and Anglo-Saxon character of construction and decoration, is best illustrated by ornaments, in which thin slabs of garnet are set upon films of diapered gold. The slabs are divided, and held in position by thin walls of gold, soldered vertically, as in cloisonné enamel, some of the Anglo-Saxon examples being decorated with elaborate filigree work, executed with marvellous accuracy and skill as regards detail. The beaded work, and cords of twisted gold, brought into play by means of the intricate convolutions of their details, is ever a subject of interest to the antiquary and the intelligent jeweller; not only from the *finesse* which characterizes the execution of the work, but for the exquisite and appropriate character of the design, which never seems to fail or exhaust itself.

The Celtic hammered work in plates of gold, of various sizes, forms, and adaptations to uses now unknown, are evidences of another kind of skill. The ornamental details are in repoussé;—vitreous pastes, amber, and rock crystal having a perfectly smooth rounded surface, or, speaking technically, cut "*en cabochon*," are also used as decorative adjuncts. Filigree and plaited work, and delicately overlaid wire ornaments, also characterized much of the Celtic jewellery, together with niello and enamel. The skill in execution and wonderful subtilty of design found in some of these ornaments discovered in Ireland and Scotland cannot be excelled: but the Oriental spirit manifested in some of the specimens is unmistakable.

Mediæval jewellery of the period from the tenth to the thirteenth century, is rarely seen except in the form of rings. These are either of great simplicity or massiveness, and frequently of both. They show little tendency to elaboration in the way of ornamental details, or any departure from the essential form necessary to the object in relation to its use.

The sixteenth century, known as the period of the *cinque-cento*, brought as great a change in jewellery, and objects of personal decoration, as in any other division of the arts. Gothic art had expended itself, but had stamped its spirit on everything of use and decoration, whether civil, military, or ecclesiastical. It had become fossilized, as it were, dead, and utterly contrary to the new condition of things which spring up with the revival of learning in Europe. All its forms and traditions had to give way before the genius of the artists of the *cinque-cento* period, men who were not handicraftsmen merely, but artists in the best sense of the word, when the jewellers' art culminated in the works of Albert Durer, Benvenuto Celleni, and Hans Holbein.

The Italian goldsmiths and jewellers of the *cinque-cento* have left such examples of their ability, as will ever continue to influence in a greater or less degree all future workers in gold. The character of the design and workmanship, at once so rich in detail, yet so light and elaborate in the mass, the exquisite arrangement and introduction of the gems employed, the beauty of the enamel, whether opaque or translucent, and the perfect adaptation of the jewels to use in connection with the rich and elaborate costumes of the period of which these jewels formed no inconsiderable portion, must ever leave the *cinque-cento* in the ascendant, as regards its decorative character and the art power displayed in its design and execution.

Of the seventeenth and eighteenth century works, very little need be said. The art became more or less mechanical, with excellence of workmanship in the accurate manipulation of the metal, the elaborate cutting of the stones, the fitting of the parts together, so as to convey the idea of a finished article, but with very little regard to the special relation which the ornament was intended to bear to, or the part it was to play in, the costume of the period. Gorgeous in the abstract, the clustered diamonds were often brought together rather for the purpose of combining a given value in some settled form, than for the purpose of utilizing the beauty of the stones for the realization of an elegant and appropriate design. The problem to be solved had altogether changed. It was no longer, " Given, a design to be realized in materials best suited to render the object a work of art suitable for wear as a personal decoration," but it was, "Given a certain number of precious stones of exceptional size and value, for the combination and construction of an ornament which, whether suitable for wear or not, should be of a fixed value in money." Fine art workmanship shrinks from the solution of such a problem, when mechanical power and skill in construction is opposed to sound taste in the realization of beauty and fitness of purpose.

It was not until after the Great Exhibition of 1851, that much attention was paid to the perfectly consistent and generic character of the Oriental design. The jewellery of the East had been up to that period regarded as only fit to be classed with the ornaments for personal decoration, used by semi-barbarous peoples in all quarters of the world. A careful examination, however, of the examples exhibited in 1851, and of others which subsequently found their way to Europe, showed that these Eastern jewellers had really laid the foundation for much of the tradition which had existed from a very early period in the goldsmiths' and jewellers' art as exercised in the West, and that, however rude or uncouth the surface finish of stones and gold work might be, the ornaments were instinct with the true spirit of decorative design. Nor could it be said that, considering the primitive means at the disposal of the workers in gold and silver, they fell below the Western workman in true skill. With an instinctive perception of harmony of colour, the primitive hue of stones, brilliantly tinted translucent enamels, filigree work, and twisted wire work, were brought to bear on jewelled constructions, in which skill of hand was only secondary to the perception of beauty that governed the production of the various objects, which Oriental tradition and custom led the jeweller to execute. It was only when under some European or other foreign influence, when the worker attempted to adapt his art to forms suited to meet Western requirements that he failed. The want of congruity between the general form as adapted to European use, and the traditionary decorative details, was fatal to success.

The traditional jewellery of Europe is best illustrated in what has been called the "Peasant Jewellery" of the various Continental nations. These vary considerably in different localities, as regards the general forms of the ornaments themselves and the character of the details, but the most ancient and genuine examples appear to be all based upon one simple mode of production, that of a thin plate of gold or silver in which the design is executed by perforations, delicate repoussé work, and the setting of stones, either real or imitation.

The custom of the ornaments of the women of one generation descending to their daughters in the next, and being handed down in families from age to age, is altogether so contrary to the modern notions of change of fashion within short periods of time, that we see at once the old and new systems are diametrically opposed to each other, and as the influence of modern change is widespread and inevitable, the preservation of specimens of the jewellery of the common people of the various countries, not only of Europe, but of the world, has been a subject which has engaged much attention since 1867, when Signor A. Castillani of Rome brought his famous collection of Italian peasant jewellery before the public in the Paris International Exhibition. This collection is now in the South Kensington Museum, classified to illustrate the various provinces of Italy; and large additions have been made during the last two or three years of specimens of French (chiefly from Normandy), Spain, various parts of Germany, Denmark, Holland, Switzerland, and finally, of the common decorations and trinkets worn by the people of India.

The study of the historic styles of ornament as applied to objects of personal decoration, together with those above quoted, as open to the student in a national museum, is of the greatest importance to the success, not only of the designer but the workman. Former methods of treatment, combinations of effect, and even, in some degree, of manipulation itself, may be suggested by the careful and intelligent examination of what has been done in the past; not so much, however, for the purposes of imitation, as to suggest a unity in the conditions of all good designs: viz. *adaptation of the object to use, the nature of the materials employed, and the handicraft, or mechanical methods, by which the design is to be realized.*

Thus far I have been dealing very briefly with the production of jewellery in the various ages and countries of the world as an art, and not as a manufacture or industry, into which a systematic division of labour enters for the purpose of economy, or to which modern science in the application of mechanical and chemical means has been brought to bear, to meet the extended and constantly extending wants of modern civilization.

With the increase of wealth, the extension of commerce, the growth of luxury, and let us hope, too, an advance in refinement, and a love of art, new wants have arisen as springing out of the old ones. These wants may take new forms, and manifest themselves when met, in new fashions; but the original sentiment is the same, and the personal decorations and jewelled adjuncts to dress of our day, stand in the same relation to the love of embellishment and ornamentation inherent in man, as it did thousands of years ago.

It is impossible to give any precise date at which the production of jewellery in its modern form commenced in Britain. It may be safely assumed that the Huguenot colony, which settled in Clerkenwell after the revocation of the Edict of Nantes, although reputed to have been chiefly watch-makers, were also producers of objects used for personal decoration. In the early and middle portion of the last century, the production of silver buckles, which formed such convenient adjuncts to the dress of the ladies and gentlemen of the period, was carried on at Clerkenwell; and there is good authority for stating that ornamental steel-work, which proved so very important an item of industry at Wolverhampton, was also carried on in Clerkenwell; and that a trade intercourse existed between Clerkenwell as the metropolitan centre of the manufacture of personal ornaments, and the provincial sources of production, Birmingham and Wolverhampton.*

The latter town was famous for the character of its artistic productions in steel, which found a ready market in London and on the continent of Europe. These works consisted of chains, chatelaines, buttons, buckles, clasps, &c. They were frequently embellished with the fine cameo-like productions of Wedgwood in blue and white jasper, or painted enamels executed at Battersea and Bilston, the latter being of a common character. Some of the more beautiful enamels were however imported from Paris, and sent back, set in exquisite mounts of steel. Sword hilts too were produced in considerable numbers at Wolverhampton. This industry came practically to an end at the period of the first French revolution. It lingered in a very attenuated form for many years, but finally died out with the skilled workers who had at one period carried it on to their own profit and the national credit.

At Birmingham, the now famous workshops of Boulton and Watt, of Soho, as also many smaller manufactories, produced considerable quantities of articles not only in steel, which seems to have been a speciality of Wolverhampton, but in gold and silver.

The production of a special kind of jewellery was

* One of the most eminent steel workers of Wolverhampton in the last century, a relative of my own, an aged man when I was a boy, told me that he commenced his industrial career in Clerkenwell about 1770, with his uncle, who was a silver buckle maker to the Court, and that from about 1780 to 1792 he had himself supplied large quantities of steel ornaments to the Courts of England, France, and Spain.

also carried on at Derby. These consisted in neatly designed pins, studs, brooches, and rings of a peculiar style of setting, still known amongst the seniors of the jewellery trade as the "Derby style." Birmingham and Clerkenwell appear to have finally divided the trade between them, so far as any organization or aggregation of industry was concerned, and in all probability this arose out of the skilled buckle makers gradually adapting themselves to changes of fashion, the new generation of workers seeking to rival the productions of foreign jewellers, or imitate those productions, when brought under their notice by the merchants whose business it was to supply the demands of distant markets.

Lapidaries to cut the stones, real or imitation, with which the buckles and buttons are frequently set; engravers, enamellers, and chasers to embellish the metal itself; solderers to put the parts together, were so many skilled workers, ready trained to the use of their eyes and fingers, and therefore as necessity arose out of a change of fashion, prepared to adapt themselves to new demands upon their skill. In addition to the buckle and button makers, there were the makers of watchkeys and seals, the latter certainly requiring the assistance of the engraver in the execution of devices of various degrees of intricacy. Intaglio heads sunk in steel were not uncommon in work executed at Birmingham in the last century.

The difference between the productions of Birmingham and London—for after all Clerkenwell is simply the jewellers' quarter of the metropolis, was much greater a few years ago than it is at present. In Birmingham mechanical appliances may be said, from the beginning of the jewellery trade, to have been essential to its success, and the various methods of stamping shapes out of thin plates of metal, as originally used in the production of steel work and buckle making, and subsequently as applied to button making (at one time the great staple of Birmingham), influenced in a large degree the methods adopted by the jewellers of that place, as distinguished from the pure handicraft system followed in London.

These mechanical methods have now been developed to an extraordinary extent, and are necessary to the success of the large concerns carried on at Birmingham; superseding as they do to a very large extent the hand labour of the past, which is reduced to a minimum in the production of articles in extensive demand. The design or pattern being once settled, the production of the article by the gross is rather a question of machinery and metal, than handicraft and skill. The accuracy of the parts as wrought out by machinery is such, that practically the articles themselves may be said to be *flung* together by the hands of those who complete them. Even elegant designs for enamelled work, as well as imitations of engraved and engine-turned surface decorations are now produced by "stamping" all the details at the same time, and by the same blow which gives the contour to the metal.

It must be distinctly understood that in thus sketching the growth of the jewellery trade as an important industry, I do not include in any sense the manufactories of high class and court jewellery, carried on to a very large extent at the west end of London, in which artistic workmen in gold are employed in the production of articles of exceptional rather than general demand. Nor must it be forgotten that there is now a large and constantly increasing demand for artistic hand-made jewellery, which is supplied by many firms in Birmingham as well as in London, and that these articles are sent to the best markets in the world. Several of these firms employ designers on their own premises; and not only at the west end of London, but in Birmingham, there are manufactories where every workman is engaged in producing an object of jewellery by hand craft, with the original design placed before him.

I have so far traced, briefly no doubt, but with a sufficiency of detail for all practical purposes, the origin and development of the manufacture of articles used for personal decoration in England. It is now desirable that the technical points necessary to an intelligent view of the nature of this industry should be considered.

The first step is to understand the nature of the material used. Of course modern trinkets, which may come to a certain extent under the generic name of jewellery, are manufactured of a great variety of materials besides gold, silver, and base metal covered with gold or silver. Of such are jet, glass in imitation of jet, tortoiseshell, bog-oak, coral, wood of varied tints, bone, ivory, and other substances. We must, however, confine our attention primarily to gold and silver ornaments, set with stones and otherwise embellished, and their imitations; treating of objects made in any other material incidentally, or as a means of illustration.

Gold in its pure state is never used in the manufacture of jewellery or plate. It is always alloyed with another metal or metals, and the quality is considered to be at once sufficiently pure, and yet well adapted to industrial purposes, when 18 parts of pure gold are combined with 6 parts of copper, copper and silver, or copper, zinc, and silver. Gold of this quality is known as 18-carat gold. French jewellery is traditionally of this standard. The English standards as indicated by the numerals stamped on objects at the Assay Offices are, 22 carats, 18 carats, 15 carats, 12 carats, and 9 carats. The latter is used in the lowest kind of manufactured jewellery, but it is only by tradition that such a quality of metal can be called gold in any true sense. Still custom does not recognize it as base metal, in the usual acceptance of that phrase.

The assay mark of much of the foreign jewellery is a very uncertain guide as to quality, because the manufacturer is permitted to secure the attendance of the officials of the Assay Offices at the manufactory, which may easily be made to cover abuses of the assay mark.

As a contrast to the character of the 9-carat gold, the standard of the English sovereign, and in fact of most gold coins, may be quoted. This is 22 carat, or only 2 parts of alloy in 24, which is really necessary to harden native gold, and make it stand the wear and tear of use as coin.

Formerly copper only was used as an alloy, and this will account for the red tint which is often seen in pure examples of old jewellery. The Dutch at one time had a special predilection for jewellery made of gold of this character. The modern use of zinc, in addition to silver, with the copper as an alloy, gives the manufacturer a great control over the tint of the metal and enables him to adapt it to the special purposes to which it has to be applied. By the use of these and other alloys, grey, yellow, red, and green tints are obtainable; which colours are sometimes introduced with great taste, in relievo groups of foliage, flowers, &c.

Gold is usually purchased by the manufacturer from the refiner, and then alloyed according to his own wants and standard. Old coin is used to a considerable extent, and the Bank of England supplies it at the rate of 3*l*. 17*s*. 10½*d*. per ounce. As the character of the alloy of gold coin is well known, whether foreign or English, its purchase is a matter of considerable convenience to the manufacturer. The gold of old jewellery, injured by wear or out of fashion, is also rendered available to a large extent, and it is feared that many exquisitely wrought historical examples of the art workmanship of past periods have found their way to the refiner's crucible through the ignorance of the possessors, or the cupidity of dealers in old gold and silver objects. Happily the demand for objects in museums has been the means of saving many an admirable example of old jewellery from the melting pot, through the fact becoming known that the bullion value was its lowest value, and that the workmanship

c 2

increased that value in proportion to its excellence and the artistic character of the design. The fact too that some of the most exquisite examples of the jewellery of the sixteenth and seventeenth centuries were so designed and wrought, that the minimum of gold consistent with strength of construction was used, prevented their being utilized as old gold, as comparatively little metal would have resulted from breaking them up. Thus the weight of metal, or at least extent of surface of metal, which will ensure the destruction of a good deal of modern jewellery when out of fashion, has, by a reverse process, saved many an exquisite jewel of past ages.

After the metal, which in any circumstances must constitute the structure of any article of jewellery, come the stones, real or imitation, with which this structure is decorated, or which may, as we shall see in due course, constitute the primary *motif* of the design. To enumerate the stones used would be simply to give a useless list, unless the leading characteristics of each could be detailed, which would be out of place here. It will be sufficient for our purpose to illustrate certain peculiarities of stones by the diamond, which, from its rarity and beauty, stands at the head of all gems when cut. Chemically it is a form of pure carbon. As a substance it is the hardest known, and can only be destroyed by intense heat. It is a popular mistake to suppose that diamonds are all colourless. A green diamond of perfect lustre is of great value alike for its beauty and its rarity. In fact diamonds are found of various colours,—blue, red, yellow, and the tints resulting from combination, and even black and opalescent.

Superficially viewed, the diamond may appear in its uncut state very much like any other crystalline substance, just as specimens of fine quartz have been mistaken for diamonds; and I may now quote some useful hints from Professor Tennant's "Lecture on Gems," as to the peculiarities of the crystalline formation of precious stones. He says: "By attending to the forms of crystals, we are quite sure that we shall not find the emerald, sapphire, zircon, or topaz, in the form of a cube, octahedron, tetrahedron, or rhombic dedecahedron; nor the *diamond*, spinel, or garnet, in that of a six-sided prism, and so with other gems. For want of a knowledge of the crystalline form of the diamond, a gentleman in California offered 200*l*. for a small specimen of quartz. He knew nothing of the substance, except that it was a bright shining substance, excessively hard, not to be scratched with a file, and which would scratch glass. Presuming that these qualities belonged only to the diamond, he considered that he was offering a fair price for the gem; but the owner declined the offer. Had he known that the diamond was never found as a six-sided prism, terminated at each end by a six-sided pyramid, he would have been able to detect the fact that what he offered 200*l*. for, was really not worth more than half-a-crown."

Diamonds are valued by weight in *carats*, the carat

being a little under five grains troy. The term is derived from the name of an African bean.

The cutting of gems is a very delicate and important operation, that of the diamond being the most difficult, from its extreme hardness and formation. It can be split by a steel tool, if the action of the tool be aimed and the blow be given in the direction of the structure. The cutting is so uncertain in its results, that diamond cutters consider the retention of one-half of the original rough diamond as a most fortunate result of the operation.

The business of the lapidary is to cut the rough gems into such forms as will best preserve their weight and enhance their brilliancy when set; and great experience, skill, and ingenuity is necessary to effect this properly. The work is long and tedious, and in the case of diamonds of large size, very costly; but still it pays for all the trouble, labour, and expense, when a pure gem is properly cut, so as to bring out its peculiarities and beauty; for this is the purpose and end of the operation.

The old English method of cutting, or rather the forms in which the stones appeared when cut, is known as the single cut, or star single cut. The present fashion results in brilliants, and double cut. A table forms the upper surface of a brilliant, while the girdle of the stone is its broadest part and is generally about a third of the depth. The bezil is that part which is above the girdle, and the base of the stone is the collet, which should be two-thirds below the girdle. The width of the stone across the girdle and the depth from table to collet, when cut, should be equal; and a little consideration shows that these agree with the generic form of the gem, an octahedron, and thus as little as possible of the material has been cut away to render it perfect as a brilliant. Roses are cut in triangular facets over the contour of the stone. The brillolette is in the form of two rose diamonds placed back to back, and is used chiefly for pendants; both sides of the jewel being required to be seen.

Pearls, which are taken from marine and fresh-water shells, are composed of carbonate of lime and organic matter. They are largely used, and have always been highly esteemed from the iridescent character of their surface. Whether employed alone or in combination with stones, thus producing contrast of colour and effect, pearls are almost invariably welcome additions in the setting of a jewel. When used, as they frequently are, in large quantities, they produce in the hands of the skilful jeweller effects which other materials fail to rival.

Cameos in shell and stone are also largely used, the latter being much more costly and desirable than the former, although the shell cameos frequently permit of great variation in the detail of the subjects treated, which may be executed with much refinement and high artistic finish. Small Roman mosaics, composed of very minute tesseræ of coloured stones, real or artificial, were formerly used to a great extent for setting in gold, but they have ceased to be much in demand.

Artificial gems or pastes are now manufactured chiefly in France, from a vitreous substance known generically as "Strass," from its inventor, a German. This so-called "Mayence base" is prepared from pure rock crystal or flint powder and salt of tartar, which, after due mixing and baking, is treated with nitric acid until it ceases to effervesce, the grit being washed until the water comes off tasteless. Fine white-lead is subsequently added, and then calcined borax as a flux. To the third stage of preparation nitre is added, and, on the mixture being melted for the last time, a crystal of a beautiful lustre is the result. Wiéland gives a base for "Strass," which is composed of silex, potash, borax, oxide of lead, and sometimes arsenic. The colouring is obtained from metallic oxides. For instance, the sapphire is imitated by using oxide of cobalt, the oriental ruby by precipitate of Cassius, oxide of iron prepared with nitric acid, golden sulphuret of antimony, and manganese calcined with nitre, with rock crystal added to the "Strass." The emerald is imitated by using carbonate of copper, glass of antimony, and oxide of cobalt, and the yellow diamond by chloride of silver and glass of antimony. Rubies are also imitated by using manganese.

These are quoted simply as illustrations of the method by which the colour of various stones is produced with the greatest success. As a primary consideration, everything depends upon the purity and excellence of the vitreous base or "Strass," which itself, when treated by the lapidary's wheel in its uncoloured state, counterfeits rose diamonds and brilliants with great success.

The production of imitation stones was carried on

with considerable success at Birmingham about fifty or sixty years ago, but under very great difficulties, by reason of the Excise laws on the glass trade. The most beautiful qualities and tints of topaz, ruby, emerald, and diamond " paste " were produced there. They are now imported more cheaply than they can be made.

Jewellery, at least in its modern treatment, may be divided into three generic sections:

1st. That in which the stones or gems are the leading features, constituting in their arrangement the design, and completing, by the effect obtained in the setting, the purpose of the jewel. The metal, gold or otherwise, is used simply as the mechanical means of fixing and arranging the gems; being practically unseen except as a means of holding the object together as a decoration for the person.

2nd. That in which the gems and gold, in combination with enamel, or engraving, or both, go to make up the design by an artistic distribution of the materials in the construction of the jewel as a whole.

3rd. That in which gold or metal alone is used, and in which the whole design is wrought and embellished by engraving and chasing, or worked perfectly plain so far as surface is concerned, the display of the metal itself being the leading feature of the design.

The modes of production have been already named as partaking of two distinct features, hand work and machinery. But a third has to be recognized, and this is the combination of hand work and mechanically produced details.

The hand-work method is the most ancient, the most legitimate, the most artistic, and, as a matter of course, the most costly; yet there are few art-industries in which the skilled worker can be said to require fewer appliances for the prosecution of his handicraft.

In Oriental countries to this day, the travelling jeweller is not unlike the travelling tinker of our own country. He carries with him all the means of executing the ornaments that he may be commissioned to make. The gold for the purposes of this work is given to him by his employer, and he squats down in some convenient position, within or outside the residence of his patron, and hammers, cuts, drills, shapes out and puts together after a somewhat rude fashion, but with an unerring instinct, ornaments which, in point of fitness to the purposes for which they are intended, and harmony of effect as regards the combination of form and colour, the Western imitator fails to approach, in spite of all the mechanical skill and scientific appliances made ready to the hand.

The Oriental worker takes the minimum of gold and other materials, and out of these he gets the maximum of effect, without any special effort to do more than give each portion of metal, each stone, and each touch of enamel, its proper position and value. He never commits the vulgarism of making a great display of gold surface, for the purpose of suggesting a bullion value which does not exist. Whatever the materials may be, rich and rare, simple or common, he makes the best of them in their integrity, from gold and gems of the purest quality and most perfect character to the most primitive imitations in glass and paste, or bits of metal foil or wood. Thus each material stands for exactly what it is, neither more nor less.

The tools and appliances necessary for a working jeweller to start in business on his own account are comparatively few, and a few pounds enables him to secure every requisite for carrying on the production of jewellery by hand. A peculiarly shaped work bench, a jet of gas, or the flame of a candle or lamp, some solder, and the inevitable blowpipe, with a vice, hammer, shears, files, punches, and drills, may be said to pretty nearly represent the plant. A few old coins, or for want of them some new ones, a few ounces of silver and zinc, and your working jeweller can commence his business, if he has skill, ingenuity, and a fair share of artistic taste. These simple elements have been the beginning of many highly successful men and important establishments.

This will account for the extent to which the working jewellers of Birmingham have spread themselves, erecting their own little workshops near to their dwelling houses, and carrying on business after a very independent and certainly respectable fashion. In Clerkenwell the same thing occurs, but in a different way, because under less favourable local circumstances and social aspects.

As a matter of course the successful workers and their descendants have become capitalists, establishing manufactories in which, although the same division of labour exists, in relation to the special articles of jewellery to which individual workmen direct their attention, yet the whole is under a general supervision and direction. Admirably arranged and well lighted and ventilated workshops, however, now take the place of the little workshop in the back yard or in the attic.

The introduction of machinery for a variety of purposes has caused a great change not only in the extent of the productions, especially at Birmingham, but in the artistic characteristics of modern manufactured jewellery.

Hand-made work of a heavy and costly character, which is now chiefly carried on in London, mostly in Clerkenwell, for the great houses at the West End which supply jewellery to the public, requires of necessity a large amount of experience, ingenuity, and skill to execute in a satisfactory manner. A design is generally made on paper, a drawing in fact representing the appearance of the article required, with sections, &c., showing the construction in cases where any novelty in that direction is aimed at. The working jeweller, taking into consideration the exigencies of his materials, proceeds to cut and shape the thin plates of gold, which in most cases is ready rolled to a suitable thickness for this purpose. He hammers, files, and punches the various portions into the requisite forms, adapting them for soldering together, or fastening by pins and rivets as may be required. In the cases where elaborate ornamental details, the human figure, or representations of animal life are required, he beats up the plate of metal to the general contour of the ornament or figure. During this operation of beating up the gold to a given shape, the metal has to be frequently passed through the fire for the purpose of annealing, otherwise it would split or crack from becoming brittle under the hammering. Filling the inside with a mixture of pitch and brickdust, he proceeds to punch and chase the details upon the surface to be finished, in the same manner as the silversmith or goldsmith works his ornaments by the repoussé process upon the surface of a vessel formed of either of the precious metals. When completed, the pitchy substance is melted out, and the detail is ready to be soldered, or otherwise fixed in its intended position.

When stones are to be set as details, or when they constitute the real basis of the design, the gold is gradually wrought to receive the stones in their proper position. The setting is never effected, as may be supposed, by being cemented into position, for the metal itself is so wrought that, after the stone is placed in its proper receptacle, the gold is closed firmly over the edges of the cut gem, holding it securely in its place.

At a comparatively recent date ready-made mountings for stones, produced by machinery, have been in use, not only in imitation but in real work. These are so contrived that the various portions of an article are cut separately and afterwards soldered together in such a manner, as to receive the stones for fixing in the usual way. A still cheaper process is also in use, consisting of a strip of metal having a serrated edge. The proper portions of the strips of metal being fixed to receive the stones, the serrations are bent over to retain them.

To set gems properly, so as to bring out all the

beauty and special features of a stone according to the cutting, requires great experience and sound judgment. The angle at which one stone is fixed in relation to another, the importance of the light being not simply refracted, but seen in transition so as to bring out the beauty of the colour, are points which require no ordinary consideration; for stones, which by one mode of setting would look very brilliant, may be made to look very commonplace by another mode.

Enamelling is largely employed in the embellishment of jewellery, to give variety of colour and contrast to surfaces. This may be described as essentially of two kinds, *champlevé* and *cloisonné*. The former is a method or system by which the enamel is applied to the surface of the metal, thus giving the details by means of a brilliant vitreous paste, which when fixed by heat becomes attached to the metal, either as an opaque or transparent body. Here again, as in the case of the manufacture of pastes or artificial stones, the metallic oxides come in as colouring substances. One species of *champlevé* enamel approaches the *cloisonné* in character, from the fact, that the enamel is fired into channels cut in the surface of the metal by the graver, these channels form a bed in which the vitreous paste is secured by the side walls of the fissures incised for the purpose, and so far serve the same purpose as the metal partitions used in the cloisonné method. This latter is of Oriental origin, and is similar to that employed with such remarkable success in the elaborate enamelled decorations of the Japanese and Chinese.

The surface to be decorated à *la cloisonné* (from *cloison*, a partition wall), is divided into sections according to the nature of the designs to be produced by the varied tints of enamel to be employed. The outline of each section is given by a wall composed of a thin piece of metal cut and bent to the proper shape, and soldered at right angles to the surface. Thus, prior to the insertion of the vitreous substance which, when fused, becomes the coloured enamel, filling up each division with its proper tint, the design is represented in outline by the thin walls of metal soldered upon the surface. After the fusion is completed, the whole is ground down to an uniform surface of metal and enamel, the metal giving a bright outline running between the various tints of colour employed.

The fusion is produced by submitting the object to be enamelled, or such portion of it as may be easily handled, to the action of a charcoal or coke fire, raised to a sufficiently intense heat inside a muffle or furnace, practically under the eye of the enameller, who watches the progress of the fusion, and regulates the application of the fire accordingly. It is needless to say that the vitreous paste which constitutes the enamel, is fusible at a much lower temperature than the metal which forms the structure of the object. Some vitreous pastes for enamelling purposes are so easily fusible, or technically so *soft* that they can be fused by a blowpipe in an ordinary candle; but these are essentially for surface decorations in colour, mostly on surfaces already covered with a coating of white enamel paste.

Enamelled details of this class are extensively used by some jewellers as a speciality; able painters in enamel, such as Essex, Bell, and others being employed to paint the subjects, which, however, have been principally heads of animals, the favourite subjects being after Landseer. The enamelling is done on gold, the name of the artist and date of the year being painted on the back of each subject. These are principally used for gentlemen's scarf pins or scarf rings. Other subjects such as classical heads painted in cameo effects are also used.

Another method of decorating the surface of jewellery is by engraving. This is largely and almost universally employed for the delicate details of modern jewellery, and is, for the most part, the result of the dexterous use of the graver. These details are the subject of careful consideration on the part of the designer and manufacturer, especially in the best class of work. The skill and dexterity with which some objects are embellished by rich diaper work and scrolls, sometimes intermingled or varied with engine turning, carried over surfaces which would otherwise present a monotonous and unsatisfactory appearance, is very remarkable. The brilliant variation of the metal, and the play of light and shadow thus introduced, without interfering with the generic form, give great art value to what might otherwise look heavy and uninteresting.

The application of machinery, and the use of mechanical appliances, other than those which have characterized the operations of the working jeweller from time immemorial, may now be considered.

As a matter of course, machinery and mechanical contrivances of an elaborate or permanent character can only be economically employed where a number of articles of the same design are required to be produced, or where the details of the article admit of repetition to a very large extent. A chain is an extreme example of the economic value of machinery when employed in its production. A brooch or bracelet is the very reverse, except where a very large number are required to be manufactured, as in the instance of imitation jewellery of a cheap class.

The first step towards a mechanical means of repetition is made, when a number of articles of the same size and design are required for the market. In that case, a die or dies are cut in steel for the exact and ready repetition of the various details which go to the making up of the design as a whole. Say, for example, the decorative gold drops to a pair of earrings. In this case the two sides of each drop will be produced from the same die, making four repetitions in a single pair. The die being cut to the design, the workman takes a thin plate of gold of the proper size, and proceeds gradually by the use of hammer and punch to drive the metal into the hollow of the die; as he does this, he has from time to time to anneal the metal, as already mentioned in the illustration of the repoussé process used in high-class hand work. Of necessity he gets a number of these plates into the same condition, anneals them, and then goes on again. Ultimately each piece of gold takes the shape of all the details, and also the surface of the *intaglio* of the die; being, in fact, a *relievo* representation of it. When completed, the two sides of the ear drop are soldered together by the use of the blowpipe, gold solder of a suitable alloy to be readily fused, and a little borax, as a flux, being employed in uniting the edges. Filed and smoothed, the proper fitting to the hooks which suspend the earring and drop to the ears has also to be accomplished by hand, the hook itself and the rosette, or other decorative detail, from which the drop is suspended, being also produced either from another die or by some other mechanical contrivance.

In this we have an illustration, so far, of mechanically made jewellery in its nearest approach to hand work. All the fitting has to be done by a skilled workman. The trained eye and dexterous manipulation are here; but the artistic production of the ornamental details is due to the die, and the dexterity with which the repoussé operation is performed by the workman. The result is an absolute repetition to any extent of the same pattern in every detail or object required. Brooches, bracelets, lockets, &c., are produced by processes like that described, the dies being adapted to the detail required, and its position in or on the object to be executed. Still the taste, skill, and dexterity in mounting these details, and fitting them with all due accuracy into their proper positions, as also the final finish of the article, are due to the skilled workman.

Ring making is as separate a branch of the jewellery trade as chain making. In the production of finger rings in numbers of the same patterns, press work is largely used, the shapes being stamped by means of a stamping press, and afterwards pressed into suitable dies much after the manner of striking a medal. Of course the preparation for setting rings with stones, &c., is largely done by hand, and the rings themselves are finished with more or less skill and minuteness according to quality and price. High class work in finger rings is however done entirely by hand, and the skill, taste, and artistic perception displayed by some ring makers are worthy of all praise. This is especially the case with the makers of "ladies'" rings, which is a separate branch of production from that of "gentlemen's" or signet rings. These latter are usually of a more massive character, requiring a totally different treatment to those made specially for ladies' wear.

So far, then, whatever of mechanical appliances the exigencies of modern manufacture have brought to bear upon the production of jewellery, in order to cheapen the labour of repetition, and meet increasing demands, very much is still left to hand work and the skill of the trained artisan, and machinery in its proper and distinct application cannot be said to play any very important part. This also may be said to apply to a considerable extent to plated jewellery, which is the best kind of imitation work. In this class of production the workmanship is altogether similar in character to that of gold, or real work, the difference consisting in the fact, that in "plated" work a film of gold covers and is mechanically incorporated with the base metal which forms the real structure of the work. The design, finish, and appearance are essentially the same as in gold work, the difference being as already stated, that between "solid gold" work as the trade terms it, and "plated," or a base metal covered with a plate of gold.

This explanation is given here, so that "plated" work may be distinctly understood as very different to a lower class of imitation jewellery which has copper for its base, and receives its gilt surface by the electro deposition of gold upon it, as a finish. In short, this constitutes the difference between imitation "plated" jewellery and "gilt" jewellery.

The application of machinery in its most legitimate and scientific form is to the production of chains of various qualities and kinds, gold, silver, and base metal. In the repetition of links, the twisting and continuous convolution of wire of varied form, machinery of most ingenious construction plays an important part; cheapening production, securing strength and flexibility, as well as beauty and uniformity, until we arrive at the manufacture of a serpent or snake chain, in which the metal is at once so attenuated, and yet possesses all requisite strength, that it can be produced in common metal at 4s. 6d. per yard wholesale! This, however, is the production of one manufacturer who keeps his own secret, which no one has at present been able to unravel.

In addition to gold work, plated, and gilt jewellery, a very large quantity of silver jewellery is made at Birmingham, and indeed most, if not all of the so-called Scotch jewellery, consisting of brooches of various sizes and kinds, shawl and plaid pins elaborately engraved, and sometimes enamelled and set with Cairngorm gems and variegated pebbles, is of Birmingham manufacture. The production of silver work is kept quite as distinct from the other branches, and in no instance, that I am aware of, are any two branches carried on by the same firm. About twenty years ago an effort was made in Birmingham to introduce, or rather revive, the production of silver filigree work as applied to various articles of personal decoration, and although some good work was done, the effort failed, and I believe that nothing of the kind is now done in England. Yet filigree presents a wide field of application, in which female labour and skill could be largely employed. The manipulation of a delicate wire, either in silver or gold, into decorative forms is a light and elegant kind of work, in which taste and ingenuity would have great scope. Possibly some turn of fashion may ere long bring it into demand; at present the filigree jewellery sold in England is of foreign production, chiefly Swiss and Italian.

The lower class of both silver and imitation jewellery is largely produced by machinery adapted to the exigencies of each particular branch. Take the lowest of all for example, as giving a full illustration. A brooch or a locket has to be produced, probably by the gross. The design being settled, and the mode of fitting the parts together so as to avoid hand work as much as possible; steel dies are sunk, not for use by hand, as in the instance already quoted, but for use in a stamping press. In addition to the die, a "force," as it is called, is also wrought by the die sinker; this fits into the die, simply allowing for the thickness of the metal which is to be mechanically pressed, or forced into it, to give it not only the requisite general shape, but every detail of ornamentation which the die sinker has executed in intaglio in the die. The front of a brooch, sides of ear drops *en suite*, &c., are stamped at a rapid rate in copper, or some suitable alloy; the two sides of a locket, with provision for hingeing and fastening, are produced in the same way, and so on throughout every kind of article which it pays the manufacturer to imitate and send into the market.

It is necessary, however, to explain, that although portions of an object having details in comparatively low relief may be stamped in the shell, so to speak, at once, yet when the relief is high this can only be done at two or three operations, the metal being annealed by fire between each process of stamping, as in the instance already quoted of the hand-wrought die, to prevent the splitting of the metal.

The finish of these articles is as rapid as their production. As they have to be gilt, science comes in when mechanism leaves them, and after "pickling" in a hot alkaline solution to remove the effects of the fire, they are immersed in the gold bath of the electro-gilder, and are quickly covered with a film of gold of greater or less density according to price. Of the attenuated character of some of this gilding, an idea may be formed from the fact that a gross of buttons is sometimes covered with three pennyweights of gold. The finish beyond this amounts to no more than giving them a shake, when dry, in a bag of bran.

It may be well to mention here a method of finishing real gold work, which has been adopted of late years with marked success. This is known as "colouring," and without in any degree giving a fictitious appearance of value to the gold, it enhances the beauty of effect. It consists of a chemical process by which the atoms of the alloy are subtracted from the surface, leaving the pure gold alone visible. It is the very reverse of gilding, which is only a film mechanically or chemically applied. Of course the "colouring" wears or becomes deteriorated by exposure; but this is a very slow process; the body of gold, however, remains the same as it was, before the colouring process was applied as a finish to the newly made object. The colouring can always be repeated, if desirable; thus renovating the surface at will.

Having recurred to real gold work, it may be as well to state here that the economical arrangements of the workshops in which both gold and silver work is made, are of such a character, as to save the metallic dust and filings, and scraps of metal, which of necessity fall about the benches and floors, and adhere to the aprons and hands of the workers. Wash-leather is largely used, especially in gold work, being soft and pliable, thus protecting one side of any object from being scratched or injured while the other is being wrought. These leathers become filled with the gold dust of the fine filings, and when so far worn as not to be available for their original purpose they are burnt in a crucible, and the gold which they have retained while in use, is found in the shape of a nodule of metal at the bottom, having been melted out of the worn out wash-leather.

The sweepings of the workshops are carefully preserved, and when accumulated are treated after a similar fashion; not usually by the manufacturer, but by persons (generally gold refiners) whose business it is to make the most of these sweepings. It is calculated that about a *pennyweight* per ounce is the average loss in hand-made work, or even two *pennyweights* in very intricate and fine work, but in machine work it is stated to be less.

So far, then, I have described the production of jewellery in its generic forms of "real" and "imitation" gold and silver work. There are, however, several other descriptions of so-called jewellery or trinkets, which may be mentioned. Notably, the bog-oak ornaments produced in Ireland, in which gold and silver work is introduced, together with stones of various kinds, chiefly a species of crystal known as "Irish diamond," as also native pearls. These bog-oak objects are all produced by hand, and often present features of considerable artistic beauty and taste.

Another kind has recently been introduced at Birmingham, which was formerly only carried on at Paris. This consists of a basis of tortoise-shell, and also imitations of tortoise-shell produced by running gelatine mixed with metallic salts, into moulds, the effect of the markings of tortoise-shell being produced by the staining with hydro-sulphate of ammonia. Horn is also used to imitate tortoise-shell, being stained and pressed into moulds while softened by heat.

The general forms of the trinkets produced in tortoise-shell and its imitations are happily limited by the conditions of the material and mode of production, and thus extravagance in outline is restrained, and the study of geometric forms becomes almost a necessity of success. In addition, however, to the decorative effect produced by the general form of the object and the colour of the material, ornamental details are inlaid in gold, silver, and gilt metal. The effect produced is generally very pleasing and artistic, when too much elaboration is not attempted: thus pretty personal ornaments are brought within the reach of persons who cannot afford the cost of gold jewellery, and yet object to wear anything in imitation of a costly material, which may look pretentious and out of keeping with their ordinary style of dress.

Coral ornaments are extensively used in a great variety of forms, but the best work is of foreign manufacture. The peculiarities of the natural growth of coral have to be studied carefully by the designer and workman, so that advantage may be taken of the formation in the production of special details adapted for setting in gold as personal ornaments. The material has ever been a favourite alike with rich and poor. The more splendid specimens in size and tint are used in the highest class of jewellery, combined with the richest and most elaborate gold setting, whilst the simple necklace of coral beads is a prize of which the peasant girl is as proud as the princess can be of the elaborated tiara. Yet both are derived from the same source, and both have that invaluable quality, which all should desire in decorative adjuncts, as in other things,—Truth.

There is only one other class of jewellery in trinkets which may be considered worth naming here, as also being *real* in itself and yet having its imitations. This is jet work. This beautiful material, so susceptible of artistic treatment in a variety of forms, is found at Whitby, in Yorkshire, in connection with the Lias rocks of the district. It appears to have been used for decorative purposes of one kind or other for a very long period. Being bright and lustrous, when cut into proper forms, polished, and properly set, it presents a very tasteful appearance, and is particularly well adapted to wear with mourning habiliments. A considerable trade is carried on in Whitby, but the mounting is chiefly executed at Birmingham and in Clerkenwell. Imitations of it are produced in glass to a very considerable extent, as also from a compound in which caoutchouc and sulphur enter very considerably, and which is known as vulcanite and ebonite. Wood powder blackened and moulded in a plastic state, and finally hardened, is also used in making imitations of jet ornaments of a cheap character. The great objection to these cheap jet ornaments is, that they have to be readily and economically mounted on plates of metal, from which, however, they are very liable to separate. The French use shell-lac as a cement, but a separation is inevitable under the changes of temperature in wearing. The English system is more permanent, and in those objects to which it can be applied, the glass and the metal are fused together by means of a foil and flux.

The social position of the artisans employed in the production of various kinds of jewellery is very superior to that of most mechanical trade employments. A certain degree of refinement and feeling for art, however uncultivated by proper art education, is a characteristic of the workmen as a class. In the higher branches this education has been brought of late years to supplement and enhance the practical skill of handcraft and the tradition of the workshop. The fact, too, that the material in which their skill and industry are employed, is of a valuable nature in itself, seems to have largely influenced them as a class, and they are trustworthy, probably from being trusted and so far relied upon by their employers. When working for themselves, the value of the material necessitates careful habits; and the foresight and precaution necessary to the prevention of waste in gold and silver would appear to give a thoughtful one to the minds of those who manufacture it. The employment too is cleanly, quiet, and somewhat sedentary, with, however, a certain activity of hands and fingers directed by brain power which lifts the worker out of the merely physical. Alike in Birmingham and in Clerkenwell, the workmen in the jewellery trades are, for the most part, respectable, intelligent, and thoughtful men, having a self respect which comes of a consciousness of responsibility and skill in relation to their daily employment, which is the best guarantee for good citizenship.

The earnings of the working jeweller are considerably above the average of the general artisan class. He must be a very indifferent workman, one in fact who has missed his vocation, who cannot earn 30s. per week, whilst the majority, especially in the higher departments of the trade in which skilled hand work and taste are required, earn from 50s. to 3l. weekly. Enamellers are a highly paid class, and earn from 3l. to 5l. per week.

In Birmingham the apprentice, who usually commences at fourteen or fifteen years of age, will earn 3s. 6d. to 4s. per week, rising to 10s. or 12s. when he is between twenty and twenty-one. A clever and industrious youth will frequently double this by *overwork*, which it pays his employer to give him.

Women are only employed in two branches, that of " guard chains," and in ordinary press work by which process the " roughs " or formation pieces of certain objects of cheap jewellery are cut out.

Certain statistics of the jewellery trade are well illustrated by Mr. J. S. Wright, of Birmingham, in a report on the jewellery and gilt toy trades of that town, prepared in 1865, on the occasion of the meeting of the British Association for the Advancement of Science, and subsequently published in a work (now out of print) on "The Resources, Products, and Industrial History of Birmingham and the Midland Hardware District." He states that in the gold chain trade "there are forty-seven master manufacturers, some employing two to three hundred hands, but the greater part not more than ten or twenty. Altogether fifteen or sixteen hundred persons are engaged in chain making, about five hundred being young women, who earn good wages, and maintain a most respectable appearance."

The same authority gives the following abstract of the number of persons engaged in the jewellery trades as a whole:

Masters	500 to 600
Jewellers proper	3000
Silversmiths	1000
Gold and silver chain makers	1500
Gilt toy makers	1000
Box makers, die sinkers, and subsidiary trades	1000
Total	7500

Recent inquiries have led me to the conclusion, from information received on trustworthy authority, that this number is now increased to ten thousand, each division having been extended in proportion, and that at the present time there is no single industry in Birmingham in which so many persons are employed.

As regards the value of the precious metals consumed annually by these trades in that town, 850,000*l.* worth is considered by those best acquainted with the subject as a low calculation, and it is probably nearer a million's worth. The value of the annual consumption of silver is calculated at 75,000*l.*

In the matter of the consumption of precious stones

we cannot give a better illustration than that afforded by Mr. J. S. Wright in the report already quoted. He says: "Forty years ago there was one stone dealer in Birmingham, and now (1865) there are thirteen. Doubtless the most valuable diamonds are set in London, but the greatest number are used in Birmingham. An ordinary manufacturer will produce earrings containing upwards of a hundred diamonds, besides a quantity of brilliants; and it is no uncommon thing for rings to be set in Birmingham with diamonds of the value of 100*l.* and upwards. Several manufacturers will keep a stock of diamonds, the value ranging from 5*s.* to 50*l.* each, and worth 1000*l.* to 2000*l.* in the aggregate." Mr. Wright then goes on to state—"a very great rise has taken place in the value of diamonds during the last twenty years, and within the last four or five years emeralds and other precious stones of fine quality have more than doubled in value. Sorts selling formerly at 3*l.* to 4*l.* per carat now fetch 10*l.* to 12*l.*; amethysts that were worth 50*s.* per ounce are now worth 8*l.* and upwards; and it is estimated that the consumption of diamonds has increased tenfold within fifteen years in Birmingham."

It will be at once conceded that with such a condition of things in 1865, values and consumption have increased during the last seven or eight years in proportion probably to the increase of the jewellery trade itself, as illustrated by the numbers already quoted.

Before concluding this very brief exposition of the present condition of the art industry under consideration, as practised at Birmingham, it may not be uninteresting to state as an illustration of its position in the middle of the latter half of the last century, that up to 1773, Birmingham had no Assay Office, and all the work done in gold and silver up to that time, had to be sent to London or elsewhere to be stamped.

In August, 1773, the Assay Office was opened, an Act of Parliament having been specially obtained to legalize such an establishment, in spite of the most determined opposition of the Goldsmiths' Company of the city of London. It was shown as an evidence of the necessity for an Assay Office, that the gold and silver work, plate and jewellery, then made in Birmingham, exceeded the total which was produced by Chester, Exeter, Newcastle, and some other less important towns, all of which had Assay Offices within their own boundaries. The course adopted by the London Goldsmiths' Company was simply that which is patent to all monopolies, which, as usual, corrected itself in due course.

It would be a perfectly hopeless task to attempt to give any statistical information as to the real extent of the jewellery trades of the metropolis. The only approximation which we can make upon a trustworthy basis, is in relation to Clerkenwell, and the figures, though derived from a well-informed source, are more or less conjectural. It must, however, be distinctly understood that the localities represented by these figures are a very considerable extension of the "Clerkenwell" of the end of the last century and commencement of the present. At the latter period, the manufactures of the district were confined within the space running from the northern boundary of the city of London, and a portion of St. Sepulchre's and the Charterhouse districts, going westward up Turnmill Street and Coppice Row, to the south side of Exmouth Street on the north, passing the vacant ground now occupied by Myddelton Street, to Northampton Square, being bounded on the east by Goswell Street and Goswell Road. Hatton Garden, from its contiguity to the City, was the place of residence of the leading people of Clerkenwell, manufacturers, and merchants, as it is now the centre of distribution; not only for the skilled trades of that locality, but for the kindred industries of Birmingham and its surrounding district.

As a matter of course, the extension of the local trades led to encroachments on districts previously free from manufactories of any kind, and now Clerkenwell industries are carried on at Pentonville and Islington.

The following figures may be taken as the nearest obtainable approximation to the numbers employed in the special branches of jewellery and kindred trades within the district indicated.

	Masters.	Workmen.
Jewellers	160	500
Goldsmiths	36	400
(Many masters use these terms interchangeably)		
Gold chain makers	33	180
Gold chasers	24	95
Forward	253	1175

JEWELLERY.

	Masters.	Workmen.
Forward	253	1175
Mourning and wedding ring makers	5	40
Engravers—seal and heraldic	12	36
Gilt jewellers	5	30
Jet ornament manufacturers	7	30
Die sinkers	12	30
Refiners	12	46
Flatting mills	4	40
Jewel case makers	22	90
Shop fitters	10	30
Total	342	1547

In thus dealing with jewellery as an art industry it was necessary for the sake of conciseness, and a proper apprehension of its importance in a national sense, to concentrate attention on the localities in which it stands out as a staple trade. Of course in most large cities, notably Edinburgh, Glasgow, and Dublin, there are jewellers as well as other workers in the precious metals, and there can be no doubt that the works executed in these places are frequently of a high character as regards workmanship, and far from deficient in the elements of sound taste.

Viewed commercially, the importance of the jewellery trade is by no means to be overlooked in the overwhelming character of the national exports generally. A large trade has sprung up with the colonies of Australia, some of which have recently imposed fiscal restrictions on personal ornaments as luxuries. The trade in jewellery with the United States would be undoubtedly very large, but for the protective tariff which effectually shields the manufacturers of Connecticut from any competition. The trade in personal ornaments manufactured in England may therefore be considered as essentially a home and colonial trade, and as regards foreign competition, it does not assume a shape in any way inimical to the best interests of the native producer; on the contrary, foreign designs tend to stimulate the ingenuity and art skill of the designer and workman, as also to provoke the competition of the capitalist and the manufacturer.

GOLD WORKING.

By Charles Boutell, M.A.

The natural qualities of the material in which the goldsmith works, when considered in connection with its preciousness, cause the expressions "gold working" and "art in gold" to be almost, if not absolutely, interchangeable terms. A highly skilled gold worker, indeed, of necessity must be an artist; and in like manner a true artist in gold will be certain to associate his mastery of his art with his practical experience as a workman. Hence, in the production of works of art in gold, between the working processes and the arts of design there exists the closest alliance. From the earliest times, also, until comparatively quite a recent period, goldsmiths' work in a signal degree has been distinguished for historical characteristics. Ancient and mediæval works in gold invariably bear the significant impress of the races by whom they have been produced, of the influences which in a greater or a less degree may have affected their national characteristics, and also of the era of their production. Thus, irrespective of all archæological considerations, the works in gold that have been bequeathed to us from past ages have their intrinsic value and their direct interest very considerably enhanced from the fact that the old goldsmiths, with unconscious fidelity, executed imperishable memorials of themselves and of their own times.

In strong contrast to the early practice of the goldsmith's art, the gold working of our own day has superseded originality by imitation; and consequently, instead of producing works of a contemporaneous historical character, we now aspire only to be reproducers of the golden legends of the past; and the works of modern goldsmiths but too generally bear the impress of the distinction between copyists and originators. With rare exceptions, indeed, even in our reproductions of early works in gold, we have attained only to an approximate degree of success, a condition of things in a great degree resulting from the want in modern gold workers of a true *feeling* for their work in its artistic character, a want which, in its turn, may be attributed to the distinction now so prevalent between the artist who designs and the worker who carries out his design. Then, again, when we have completely mastered the old processes, we constantly fail in their application, through inability thoroughly to sympathize with the old workers in associating processes with motives, the means for working, with the objects to be attained by the work when done. On the other hand, during the last few years a very great advance unquestionably has been achieved towards a high standard of excellence in modern gold working, a satisfactory and also an encouraging fact, which has been brought about, first, by a general hearty recognition of the supremacy of the early goldsmiths as masters of their craft; and, secondly, by a judicious selection of the best of the early schools and masters to furnish authorities to be studied, and models either for direct reproduction or variously modified suggestion. Whatever may be in store in time to come for works executed in the most precious of the metals, this much is certain, that for a while the great aim of our gold workers, including in their ranks the ablest of their fraternity, must be, to become sound archæologists, since for a while we must be content to produce archæological gold work; if possible, such gold work as may fairly take rank with the original productions of centuries that have long passed away. When the gold workers of those past times shall have found rivals in their successors of to-day, then, and not till then, may we contemplate such a forward step as may lead to originality in our own works in gold, and consequently we may hope to endow them with contemporaneous historical attributes, that will be both truthful and significant.

If himself a true artist—and, as already has been observed, a true artist, a master of the goldsmith's craft of necessity must be—the modern worker in gold will not need to have impressed upon him the extreme importance of preserving in his own works the distinctive characteristics of his models from various schools and periods, so as to avoid any approach towards confounding the teachings of essentially different styles and of successive eras. Thus, in our reproductions of the early goldsmiths' works, we should aspire to work so heartily in harmony with their spirit, that their designs might appear to belong to ourselves and that our works might have been accepted by them. In one of not the least valuable of their qualities, it will be well for the goldsmiths of all ages to follow closely in the footsteps of their fellow-craftsmen of olden times. This is, in acquiring and giving expression to a perfect knowledge both of what *can* be done and of what *ought* to be done with gold as a working material. From its extreme intrinsic beauty and delicacy, as well as from the ease with which it may be worked, combined with its imperishable nature, gold far surpasses all other materials for the noblest efforts of the modeller and the engraver; while, at the same time, it maintains a corresponding supremacy when used by artists of less exalted rank for the production of a numerous variety of objects, in which practical utility is blended with artistic grace and beauty. Still there exist limits that may be accurately defined to the legitimate and consistent applicability of gold, as there are classes of objects altogether unfitted for production in this regal metal. In all cases also it ought carefully to be kept in remembrance, that the preciousness of this material, which lends an additional charm to true works of art, degenerates into a mere element of vulgar display in unworthy objects, or in designs, devoid alike of taste and effectiveness, which are unable even to claim the merit of skilful execution.

Notwithstanding the serious drawbacks to complete success in the higher departments of their craft, arising from the inability to exhibit independent originality of design, experienced by our workers in gold, it happily is true that they manifest unmistakable signs of being generally impressed with the conviction of wielding what really and truly is an art; an art, too, which, in consequence of the almost universal diffusion of works in the precious metals, in a pre-eminent degree is qualified to exercise a powerful refining and elevating influence upon the public taste. This fact is exemplified in a conspicuous manner in the productions of our own goldsmiths. Accordingly it has become rather the rule with them than the exception in their practice, not only that they take into consideration the nature of the object they have to produce and the purpose or use for which it is to be applied, but also that they attach great importance to beauty of form, purity of style, and consistency in either richness or simplicity of decoration. At any rate, our goldsmiths, reversing the principle laid down in the Jury Report on the precious metals of the London International Exhibition of 1862, to the effect that producers "as much as possible should draw their inspirations from their customers," are beginning to feel, that their own success mainly depends upon their displaying such artistic powers as may enable them to guide and instruct their patrons, instead of being led and governed by them. As a matter of course, it may be assumed to be the aim of our best gold workers, with the highest possible artistic excellence to combine the most complete utility. In this combination, however, the master goldsmith will always have Nature before him as his model and instructress, teaching him and showing to him that, as in her works, so in his own, the useful and the beautiful are not to be regarded as distinct elements, but, on the contrary, as being so intimately blended together that the utility of any object is enhanced by the very beauty which is a part of itself, its beauty being essential to the completeness of its usefulness.

The processes and operations which are employed in gold working and contribute to the production of goldsmiths' work, are both numerous and varied. They may be divided into two primary and principal groups, the one of them being chemical and the other being mechanical. The works bequeathed by them to our own times prove the gold workers, not only of the middle ages but even of a remote antiquity, to have attained to a very high proficiency in both these divisions of the means and appliances for the practical exercise of their craft. The grand achievements of modern science, indeed, can claim to have done very little, if they have done anything at all, to strengthen the hands of the goldsmith of to-day; certainly they have not enabled him, in many of the more subtle and delicate expressions of his art, to advance beyond the attainments of his early predecessors. Without hesitation or reserve, I have been told by the living goldsmith who stands first and foremost among the brethren of his craft, Signor Alessandro Castillani, of Rome, that our age has witnessed— rising, as if by magic, from the cemeteries buried out of sight and of remembrance long before Rome came into existence — the discovery of various kinds of objects in gold of a workmanship so exquisite, that not only has it been a matter of extreme difficulty for the most experienced and skilful of modern gold workers approximately to imitate them, but for a considerable time it was not possible even to explain theoretically the processes, whether scientific or mechanical, that had been employed in producing them. Experiments, researches, efforts of every kind, all of them long carried on in every direction and with an invincible perseverance beyond all praise, for a while resulted only in failure, except so far as went to add fresh confirmation to the already palpable fact that the ancient goldsmiths were acquainted with both chemical and mechanical agents that were unknown to modern art and modern science, and that they used those agents with a masterly ability and skill that was absolutely marvellous. The ancient processes of melting and soldering gold, of wire-drawing, and of separating and joining firmly together minute particles of the precious metal scarcely perceptible to the naked eye, and thus giving to the work so produced a delicate and yet rich granulated aspect, were all equally problems. Further and still more searching experimental investigation proved these ancient processes to be essentially different from those practised in the most celebrated schools of modern gold workers throughout Europe. At length a fortunate chance led the indomitable inquirers to discover among the mountaineers of Calabria a race of peasant workers in gold who still retained, under rude conditions, certain hereditary traditions which proved to be the key which should lay open the long-hidden secrets of the Italo-Greek goldsmiths of pre-Roman antiquity. Then the clue, once found and its fidelity certified, was carefully and thoughtfully followed along its entire length; the old workmanship once more was wedded to the old art;

the Signori Castillani in triumph reached the goal of retrogression, and became qualified for stamping their works, produced in the second half of this nineteenth century, with whatever symbol might have done duty as "Hall mark" in Italy about the year 1000 B.C.

The remarkable discoveries of the Signori Castillani and their practical triumphs have acted as powerful incentives and encouragements to the more enterprising goldsmiths of our own country and on the continent of Europe, especially to those of Denmark, to follow where the eminent Italians led the way. And if the Castillani still are able to maintain their supremacy as scientific goldsmiths, here and there their example has proved effectual in attracting fellow-craftsmen to approach near to them, in attaining at any rate to a comparative mastery of the science of gold working. Our own gold workers also may justly claim to have in their ranks numerous masters in manipulative skill; in fact, it is but too decided a characteristic of our existing system of working in the precious metals, that in manual skill and dexterity our practical goldsmiths are very strong, while in both the science and the art of their craft they are comparatively weak. At present it must be admitted, with rare exceptions, that even the best modern goldsmiths' work, as compared with ancient work of the same order, is more mechanical and less scientific. The introduction, too, and the use of machinery for the production of artistic and decorative goldsmith's work, with the express object of reducing the cost of workmanship by superseding hand work as far as possible, however excellent in itself this machinery may be, and practically effective as its mechanical action unquestionably is, of necessity implies a formal precision in its productions and a minutely uniform exactness, altogether incompatible with that freedom and expression which can be imparted only by the touch of the craftsman's own hand. That various mechanical agencies should be employed by gold workers must be accepted as a matter of course, precisely as it must be desirable for them to seek in the mechanical agencies in their employment the highest attainable degree of excellence; at the same time, the true goldsmith never will fail to regard all discoveries in chemical science and all improvements in tools and machinery, merely as means better qualified than before, for enabling him as a workman to realise his conceptions and to give expression to his feeling as an artist.

Without attempting exact accuracy on such a question, and leaving a wide margin for additions from unexplored or only partially explored regions, including a vast portion of China, the total quantity of gold in use, or in a condition at once to be made available for use in the world, may be estimated to be equal to about 1,150,000,000*l*.—about eleven hundred and fifty millions sterling, an amount which, not including any item to represent workmanship, is merely the probable value of the metal itself. Of the total production of gold, careful investigations have led to the conclusion that somewhat more than one-third is absorbed in coinage. A reserve of unemployed gold, held in ingots, &c., by bankers, or hoarded in some form or other by private individuals, accounts for about five per cent. of the whole amount. The yearly loss occasioned by waste and wear and tear, of which it would scarcely be possible to form even an approximately correct estimate, must account for another by no means inconsiderable percentage. Thus upwards of one-half of the entire production of gold remains for consumption in the arts and in the manufacturing industries of different countries, together with export for miscellaneous objects and purposes, of which no specific account is obtainable. Of the gold consumed in the arts and the manufacturing industries, the quantity must be very large that is used in the various processes of gilding—as frame-gilding, electro-gilding, water-gilding, the ornamentation of ceramic works, bookbinding, the interior and also the exterior decorations of buildings, and other like processes. Photography also absorbs gold in a continually increasing degree. All this absorption of the metal takes place in almost every part of the civilized globe; and the gold thus employed may be considered so far to be practically lost, that it cannot be available for use either under other conditions or for any different purpose, or again under the same conditions or for some similar purpose. Without being thus practically lost for ulterior objects, gold is in constant use in large quantities for the manufacture of cases for watches; also in the form of thread or wire, it is employed to a considerable amount in making gold-lace and in connection with many other textile manufactures. Upon the great consumption of gold for the production of personal ornaments, and especially of chains, it will be enough here to remark that the metal thus used, for the most part, remains in our own country or finds its way to our own colonies, the exports of British-made gold jewellery to foreign countries being comparatively small.

By his workmanship the goldsmith increases the value of gold, on an average, to the extent of 60 per cent. This increase of value in gold itself, however, rises in proportion to the degree in his art to which the gold worker himself has attained, so that the intrinsic worth of the precious metal in which he works may be decidedly subordinated to the higher value that it may acquire at the hands of the craftsman. The pure metal, it must be added, in consequence of its softness, is not used (except by some Indian and African workmen) in the production of objects of whatsoever kind, the nearest approach to unalloyed purity in the metal being in the standard of our own coinage, which fixes the admixture of alloy with the native gold as in the proportion of 2 to 24—one-twelfth, that is, of the whole. Goldsmiths consider gold, whatever the form or weight of any mass or particle of the metal, to be divisible—or to be accepted as divisible—into twenty-four equal parts, each part being denominated a "carat." And as this term also is assumed to be applicable only to the pure native gold, the proportion in which the unalloyed metal is present in any object is expressed in its carats, the proportion of the alloy being understood to be intimated in the number of parts required to complete the aggregate of twenty-four. Thus the gold of the coinage—and the gold of wedding-rings shares its standard with the coinage—is "22 carat," inasmuch as in this standard, twenty-two parts of pure gold are present in combination with two parts of alloy. In like manner the "18 carat gold" of our best and most valuable goldsmiths' work, which is found to be most advantageously adapted for working, and at the same time is held to be sufficiently pure to have a just title to rank as truly "precious metal," has eighteen parts of pure gold and six parts of alloy, composed either entirely of silver, or of silver and copper in varying proportions, or of silver and copper with an admixture of zinc; these variations in the composition, and consequently in the chemical character and action, of the alloy, enabling the gold worker to give various tints to the compound metal in which he works. By the introduction of some other alloys, a still greater range of hue and tint may be imparted to the gold when prepared for actual service. Compound metals, when used in goldsmith's work, continue to be entitled and estimated as "gold," when they are "15 carat" (fifteen parts gold and nine alloy), "12 carat" (one-half gold and one-half alloy), and even "9 carat" (nine parts gold and fifteen alloy), or the reverse of "15 carat gold."

The quality of native gold, in a great degree, is determined by the locality from which it may have been obtained; not only does the time vary in which it can be brought into a condition suitable for working, but various means have also to be adopted before the desired result can be obtained. Sometimes the operation of smelting has to be repeated not less than ten or twelve times; and fluxes, or chemical agents endowed with certain active properties, have to be employed in order to expel those foreign substances with which the workers know well how to deal. The smelting and purifying having been accomplished, the admixture of the alloys succeeds; after which, the metal, then in a condition ready for the gold worker, is cast into flat skillets or ingots of square section, preparatory to being rolled down by machinery to whatever thickness or tenuity may be required for plates or wires. Occasionally, but on rare occasions only, the artist in gold sculptures his work from out of the block of precious metal. Again, without recourse having been had to any rolling down, objects in gold are often cast in moulds, to be finished by the hand of the artistic gold worker with a fine chisel, or a finer burin, and with various chasing tools. The gold worker also calls to his aid the lathe with its manifold accessories; he employs acid for biting-in; he uses punches and stamps of various kinds; servants of great value and infinite versatility he finds ready to his hand in intaglio steel dies of every imaginable form; and last, and best of all, the hammer is the instrument with which in his repoussé work he accomplishes his noblest achievements. The blow-pipe, it is scarcely necessary to add, the gold worker has ever near at hand, in order to enable him with prompt efficiency to invoke the active and never-failing co-operation of his great ally, the element fire. When in thin plates, the gold is first cut into the desired forms, and then either punched out and beaten, so as to obtain whatever of the design would not have to depend upon the final chasing and engraving for the completion of the finished object. As it must generally be the case, that works to be executed in gold of necessity should actually be made in two or more parts, these parts when completed are "mounted," or united, either by soldering or riveting, the latter process being generally restricted to those parts of works which are comparatively of large size. Soldering is a process, upon his mastery of which in a signal degree depends the success of the worker of gold. It is here that the science of gold working accomplishes its most excellent triumphs, by enabling the craftsman to form a single object from very many parts, some, if not all of them, of minute size; the combination of the whole, both in security and perfect adaptation, being productive of effects not otherwise to be obtained. It was in the peculiarity of their soldering, indeed, and its perfection, that the ancient Italo-Greek goldsmiths so long kept at bay the ablest and most enterprising of their modern successors; and it was not until he had the good fortune to penetrate the mystery of the soldering, that Castillani was able to give to his gold work that exquisite granulated surface, firm as solid metal, which for delicacy and effectiveness knows no rival. In this beautiful and truly wonderful granulated work the gold is absolutely *pulverised*, and the minute particles are subsequently united, as clusters of needles or as steel-dust might be upon a magnet, the solder fixing them in complete union, each particle still retaining its own individuality. In England, the goldsmiths who, in their granulated gold work, have approached nearest to their distinguished Roman fellow-craftsmen, are the Messrs. Phillips, Brothers and Son, of Cockspur Street, London, gentlemen who also are second to no living goldsmiths in the production of works in gold designed in the various styles of ancient and early art. In the front rank of archæological goldsmiths other places are occupied by the Messrs. Brogden and Watherston, all of London, who also enjoy a very high reputation as makers of gold chains. For the production of Scandinavian archæological goldsmith's work, Mr. Borgen, of New Bond Street, himself a Dane, who for many years has been established in London, is *facile princeps*. Mr. Borgen also has successfully introduced into this country the production of delicate gold filigree, executed by Danish craftsmen who have settled in London, the designs always being derived from existing Scandinavian relics of some one of the earlier centuries of the middle ages. It is to be hoped that this beautiful and effective application of fine gold wire may speedily attain to a recognized position among us, as one of the popular modifications of gold working considered as a British industry.

In addition to employing at his discretion, either singly or in combination, the different processes directly connected with working the precious metal itself by means of every one of which agencies he is enabled to impart to gold a fresh value through its alliance with art, the goldsmith, in certain closely allied artistic processes, has at his disposal other facilities, not indeed for "gilding refined gold," but

F

for enhancing its beauty and still further increasing its preciousness. Foremost among these processes which are in legitimate alliance with the primary operations of the gold worker is the beautiful art of enamelling, now practised in England with great success. The term "enamel" strictly is applicable only to several coloured vitreous substances that are attached to the gold by fusion; the same name, however, is in general use to denote the enamelled metal. The colouring bodies obtained from metallic oxides, or "salts," which before their application to the metal are mixed with certain vitreous mineral fluxes easily fusible, for their true and permanent effect depend altogether upon heat at a high temperature, to which they are exposed when they are enclosed in the muffle-furnace. At one and the same time, heat melts the fluxes and develops the colours of the oxides, giving them their brightness and brilliancy, and also incorporating them with the goldsmith's work which they will adorn. This has to be accomplished by means of a series of successive "firings," each of them attended with various perils to the works that are thus passing through their probationary career; and all of them causing anxiety to the craftsman, while he maintains a vigilant watch over the action of the furnace, and is kept in suspense, until the result of the final "firing" shall have determined the true character of his work. In the early opaque enamels, opacity was obtained by adding to the vitreous compound mass oxide of tin; but modern enamellers use various other chemical agents to give opacity to different enamels. Full

particulars on these points are given by Dumas in his
'*Traité de Chimie appliquée aux Arts*;' in the '*Traité
des Couleurs pour la Peinture en Email*' of Montany,
and in the work bearing the same title by Neri: also in
Reboulleau's '*Nouveau Manuel de la Peinture sur Email*.'
The two groups into which "Encrusted Enamels"
are divided will be found described in the accompanying treatise on "Jewellery;" further general
description of them here therefore is unnecessary. In
enamels encrusted by the "Champlevé" process, the
coloured portions of the work are frequently restricted
to the background; and thus the figures and other objects of each composition, whether executed in relief or
not, have their golden surfaces untouched except by
the burin and the chasing tools. A distinct class of
enamels is occasionally employed by modern goldsmiths for adornment of some of their more costly
works. These enamels, instead of being *applied* to a
metallic base, are *inserted* in openings pierced through
the gold for their reception, and consequently they are
set clear, with a view to having their full effect displayed when held up to the light. Of these translucent enamels, distinguished by the early enamellers as
"Émaux de plique à jour," which may be considered
to represent gems set under similar conditions, a few
remarkably fine examples were exhibited by French
goldsmiths at the great artistic and industrial gathering at Paris in 1867. Other varieties of enamels are
those which, being translucid, are *painted* upon gold
work in relief with engraved outlines; and true painted
enamels, which came into use towards the close of the

F 2

fourteenth century, and by which *pictures*, properly so called, *in enamel* are produced. These pictures, which the fire burns into, being imperishable, put to the severest test both the skill and the patience of the enamel painter; for his work then is done only when his picture for the last time shall have left the furnace. As he paints, he can at best but anticipate the aspect that he desires and expects his work to assume as it passes through the fire; since the colouring substances which he uses in the process of painting are not colours at all, but pastes having a generally uniform dull appearance, their actual colours being latent in their chemical nature until stimulated by exposure to a high temperature into a condition of visible and vivid activity. Of living enamellers on gold the foremost place of honour must be assigned to M. Charles Lepec, of Paris, a considerable number of whose finest and most precious works happily have found permanent homes in our own country. In Westminster Abbey we possess the finest early example of heraldic *champlevé* enamel known to be in existence— it is the shield, charged with his armorial insignia, attached to the left arm of the effigy of William de Valence, first Earl of Pembroke, A. D. 1296; the base of the enamel, however, here is gilt copper, the gilding having been produced by an amalgam of melted gold and mercury, fixed at a moderate temperature which would not affect the incrustations.

Damascening, a decorative art in favour with goldsmiths, was successfully practised by the ancients, and was also retained in use during the middle ages, but it was always more prevalent in the East than among the nations of the West. Specially famous in the Levant, this art is considered to have obtained its distinctive title from the perfection to which it was carried by the early goldsmiths of Damascus. It was introduced into Italy in the fifteenth century, and there attained to its highest excellence in the sixteenth. This damascening consists in imbedding wires or threads of gold or silver, so forming various designs and devices, upon some less brilliant metal, as iron or bronze, the entire work being finished with a uniform level surface; or damascening may be executed by imbedding gold wires upon silver, or silver wires upon gold, and highly attractive effects thus may be obtained. Some excellent damascening is now produced in the establishment of Mr. Barkentin, a Danish goldsmith, for many years established in London. Damascening, however, exclusively executed with the precious metals is but little practised in England.

Niello, another decorative art applied effectively to goldsmith's work, like damascening, may be considered naturally to have resulted from the practice of the illustrious art of engraving—engraving by the burin, that is, for the purpose of producing surface decoration upon objects executed in metal, and without any view to the application of engraven plates for multiplying copies of "engravings" by impression. Transmitted from an early antiquity to the middle ages, Engraving by mediæval artists was chiefly practised by goldsmiths and armourers, who were both accomplished draughtsmen and skilful in the use of the burin. These artists constantly filled in their engraved lines with a black enamel-like substance, which gave emphasis to the engraven compositions, precisely as they also at other times sought corresponding results by incrustations of gold or silver threads. Thus Niello and Damascening are sister arts, the offspring of the same parent art, Engraving. To the excellence of the nielli of Maso Finiguerra, the pupil of Ghiberti and Masaccio, who flourished in the middle of the fifteenth century, and to the magnificent indirect results to which they accidentally led the way, it is unnecessary here to make more than a passing reference. At the same time it is not possible to withhold the expression of a desire to see niello, which in Russia is both in general use and executed with remarkable success and excellent effect, rising in the estimation of British goldsmiths. It will be well indeed for our own workers in gold in all things to emulate their predecessors in seeking to raise their craft to the highest attainable rank, by elevating the standard and extending the range of their own powers as artists, as men of science, and as craftsmen. In his famous treatise, '*Diversarum Artium Schedula*,' Theophilus has devoted seventy-nine chapters of his third book to enabling us to form a true estimate of the varied information and the eminent ability of the master goldsmiths, his own contemporaries, of the twelfth century. We ought to have men of the same order among ourselves. It may be, and doubtless it is, true, as Signor Castellani has declared that true it must be, that for a while in our gold-working we still must rest content to be successful—

assuming that we are able to become successful—imitators of the great goldsmiths of ages which have passed away; yet it by no means follows that our own goldsmiths are to consider their horizon to be finally closed in within the bounds of masterly imitation. There is a wide field lying open beyond this border-land of reproduction, to which our gold workers are bound to look forward, and which, if true to themselves and their craft, they will trust in due time to reach. The first step in this direction of advance was taken when the most distinguished goldsmiths of to-day, having given an unreserved recognition to the masterly abilities of their far-off predecessors, declared themselves to be humble learners from them; the next step will be taken in the same direction when these learners, having become their masters' equals, will be independent masters themselves.

WATCHES AND CLOCKS.

By F. J. Britten (British Horological Institute).

In proportion to the number of watches and clocks imported into this country, but few of home manufacture are produced; a somewhat remarkable fact, considering that England has been the source of nearly every important invention in connection with the improvement of timekeepers, and that in most of the mechanical arts she has held her own against the world.

The high estimation in which English watches were held in the latter part of the last century, induced by the admirable and artistic productions of Tompion, Graham, Mudge, and other conscientious makers, received a shock from the wholesale forgery of eminent names upon worthless goods by dishonest speculating manufacturers, who swamped the best English markets with their frauds, until in 1816 a committee of the House of Commons was appointed, on the petition of the London and Coventry watchmakers, to take evidence respecting the lamentable state of destitution to which the petitioners were reduced, in consequence of a diminution of their trade. There appears but little doubt that these spurious and valueless watches were far greater in number than the genuine works of the acknowledged English artists, and that their distribution so damaged the reputation of English watchmakers, that the Swiss, who had adopted Graham's cylinder escapement for their watches, were enabled to take possession of our foreign markets without much difficulty, and even to compete with us in our own country. They are now our most formidable rivals in the production of cheap watches, and adhere to the cylinder escapement for the great bulk of their manufacture, although it does not furnish exact results and has been long discarded by English watchmakers, who are still distinguished by the love of their art, and the desire to attain perfection which actuated Tompion and Graham.

With the introduction of railways and the adoption of Greenwich time as the standard throughout the country, exactness in recording time became more than ever necessary; and yet the large demand for timekeepers which arose as railways were opened, was in a great measure met by Swiss watches and American clocks, low in price, and with but little pretence to accuracy. The numerous delays and accidents arising from unpunctuality, and the anxious uncertainty as to the time on the part of those who have precise engagements, afford ample testimony that our means of showing the standard of time are still deficient. Not only are the majority of clocks very bad and misleading, but opportunities of comparing timekeepers with the standard are wanting. In this respect England is behind some other countries, and London even worse off than many provincial towns. Our public clocks differ several seconds and often minutes, but the variation is viewed with complacent indifference by most people, although it involves an alarming waste of time and risk of accident which is quite unnecessary.

Some years ago the Council of the British Horological Institute, with the countenance and assistance of the Astronomer Royal, endeavoured to induce the Corporation of London to provide public clocks controlled from Greenwich Observatory, and so lately as the latter end of 1874 Sir Edmund Beckett, the President of the Horological Institute, asked the Postmaster-General to cause the time signals now sent to the post-offices to be exhibited in the windows, but without effect. It is owing to this want of appreciation of correct timekeeping that so many people purchase worthless clocks and toys called watches of foreign manufacture, to the serious detriment of the English trade. An army of watch and clock jobbers throughout England spend their lives in pottering over these precious articles, endeavouring to keep their mechanism moving, at the expense of their unwise owners. Messrs. De la Rue and Co., the one firm unconnected with watchmaking who receive the correct time from Greenwich by means of a controlled clock, estimate that it saves them 300l. a year. Good English watches are robbed to a great extent of their value for want of correct standards, the possession of which would greatly benefit the English trade and increase the nation's wealth by an incalculable saving of time.

Clockmaking and watchmaking, although nearly allied, are two distinct industries, and must be considered separately, with a view to some chronological arrangement. I will first glance at the various stages of clocks and other non-portable timekeepers.

The necessity of being able to record the progress of time at lesser intervals than a day, even in the most primitive state of mankind, and the apparent suitability of the means by which the world is divided into day and night for attaining that end, place the first attempt to make the motion of the earth available for registering the subdivisions of days, beyond the reach of history.

The sundial of Ahaz, mentioned in the second book of Kings, is the first on record; and although called a sundial in the English version of the Bible, it is supposed by commentators to have been merely a stair formed so that the shadows of the steps expressed the hours and the course of the sun. Evidence exists that the famous obelisks of the Egyptians were intended as gnomons; but the earliest sundial of which we have any definite description is the hemicycle or hemisphere of the Chaldæan astronomer Berosus, who probably lived about 540 years before Christ. No doubt sundials were used both by the Greeks and the Romans. Among the Elgin collection in the British Museum, there is a dial with four faces, which it is conjectured was intended to show the hour at one of the crossways at Athens, in which city it was discovered.

The clepsydra or water clock appears to be the first contrivance for measuring spaces of time, independently of the motion of the earth. It is of great antiquity among Eastern nations. Although no date can be assigned for its invention, there is evidence that it was introduced into Greece by Plato. The varied forms in which water clocks have been found testify to the great amount of ingenuity expended in their production through many ages. At the present day there is one in use at the Royal Observatory, Greenwich.

Some of the varieties of the clepsydra would naturally suggest to a mechanical mind the idea of obtaining the necessary motive force for a machine to mark time, by allowing gravity to act upon some body other than water, so that it is not surprising to find men of known ingenuity, from Archimedes before the Christian era, to Gerbert, a monk who lived at the end of the tenth century, named with confidence as the inventors of clocks composed of wheels actuated by a weight. The earliest clock, however, worthy of the definition, the details of which are on record, is that made by Henry de Wick for Charles V. of France, in the tower of whose palace it was placed about the year 1368. Rude as it undoubtedly was, for it had an hour hand only, Henry de Wick's machine furnished the basis for our present turret clocks, and deserves a brief description. A heavy weight being tied to a rope, which was wound round a cylinder or barrel, served as the power to cause the hand to revolve; but the hand, instead of being fixed to the axis of the barrel, had its motion communicated through several toothed wheels, called a train of wheels, arranged in such a manner that the hand made several revolutions for one revolution of the barrel, so that the weight did not need to be wound up so frequently. If the weight were allowed to freely act upon the hand, its motion would have been accelerated, so that what is now known as an escapement had to be devised, whereby all the spaces traversed by the hand should be accomplished in equal time. Attached to a vertical axis were two arms, each carrying a weight; upon the same axis were two spikes or pallets, at right angles and apart from each other a distance equal to the diameter of the last wheel in the train; the teeth of this wheel were formed on its side instead of its periphery. One of the pallets projecting in the path of the wheel teeth had to be pushed aside before the wheel could revolve. The tooth, in turning the pallet round its axis, had to overcome the inertia of the weight hung upon the arm; and the arms having notches in them to allow the weights to be removed farther from or nearer to the centre of motion, the operation of pushing the pallet on one side could be arranged to occupy the required time. But having succeeded in getting clear of one pallet, the progress of the wheel was barred by the second pallet, which would, in its turn, be presented to the tooth on the other side of the centre, and in being thrust aside, would carry the arms and weights in an opposite direction. The whole process being continually repeated, resulted in a constantly alternating motion of the arms and the weights attached, whereby the motion of the hand was kept tolerably uniform.

Not only has a reciprocating motion of matter been used ever since for controlling the motive power of timekeepers, but the very mechanism employed by De Wick held its own for many years, under the title of the verge escapement. Most of the parts of De Wick's clock were of iron, and it had an arrangement for striking, similar to that which is often seen in many of the foreign clocks of the present day. The work must have been rough, but it was a distinct achievement, for although springs were introduced as motive power and other inventions made with the view to render clocks portable, no real stride towards perfection in timekeeping seems to have been accomplished for more than two centuries. The celebrated Strasbourg clock, made about 1370, by Conradus Dasypodius, may be mentioned as a wonderful piece of mechanism, but it cannot be instanced as an attempt to measure time with greater exactness. Records exist of many curious applications of clockwork, such as it was, but except so far as finer work and slight alterations, such as screwing the weights on the arms instead of hanging them on the timekeepers, were almost exact copies of De Wick's.

In 1631 the clockmakers of the city of London were incorporated as a company, and obtained their charter from Charles I. This affords substantial evidence that the art of clockmaking then flourished as an English industry, and from that time to the present day nearly every important advance in the principles of machines for measuring time may be traced to the genius of Englishmen.

The application to clocks of the pendulum may be regarded as the first real improvement on De Wick's principle. It is unnecessary to reproduce the well-worn account of Galileo's discovery published in his treatise in 1639, which led to the use of the pendulum by astronomers for recording the time of observations. The first idea of its application to the clock then in use was doubtless to turn the axis of the balance to a horizontal direction, cut off one of the arms, and let the remaining weight answer the purpose of the pendulum-bob. As it is requisite, however, that the pendulum in vibrating shall describe a cycloidal curve, if all its oscillations are to be performed in the same time, no matter what the length of the curve travelled through, the result would not be satisfactory, for it is a necessity of the verge escapement that the pallet axis shall describe nearly 90 degrees, and in such a range the circular arc described by the bob would differ very materially from a cycloidal curve. There appeared two ways to surmount the difficulty, viz. by inventing an escapement which should allow the pendulum to vibrate so small a distance that its path would not sensibly differ from a cycloid, or, while keeping the verge escapement, to introduce some contrivance to cause the pendulum to trace the desired curve. By a common fatality, the latter, and (as experience has taught) totally impracticable method was adopted.

Huyghens, a French clockmaker of eminence, about 1650, showed great skill and ingenuity in arranging pendulums to clocks, so as to describe a cycloid. The most favoured device was, to make the upper part of what would have been the pendulum rod, either of a steel spring or of a cord, which in its travel should press against plates bent to the desired curve and placed one on either side. Detaching the pendulum from the pallet axis, and hanging it independently, was the first step in the right direction. It is worthy of notice, that the steel spring, shortened and freed from the cycloidal checks, has been found to be incomparably the best plan for suspending the pendulum. However, no good result attended the endeavours to keep the path of the pendulum a cycloid, and it remained for Robert Hooke, born at Freshwater, Isle of Wight, to solve the difficulty by inventing the anchor escapement, with which the pendulum need only travel a very short distance, say about two degrees. Although the question was now satisfactorily settled, and experience showed the cycloidal path to be practically unnecessary, yet for generations people were to be found wasting time and money in contriving all sorts of useless cycloidal checks and methods of lengthening and shortening the pendulum during its vibrations. The chief difference between Hooke's anchor escapement and the dead-beat escapement of Graham, to be presently described, is, that the pallets were so shaped in Hooke's anchor escapement, that the pendulum towards the conclusion of each vibration and just before receiving impulse from the train, pushes it backward. This recoil of the train may be observed in the seconds' hands of old English eight-day clocks fitted with this escapement, which recede during what would otherwise be their intervals of rest.

At the end of the seventeenth century, George Graham perfected Hooke's escapement, by making it so that the recoil in the train was obviated. Many authorities at the time asserted the recoil to be an advantage, and even essential for accuracy of time-keeping, by its tendency to keep the vibration of the pendulum constant, a result much better attained by increasing the weight of the pendulum bob.

In spite of suggested alterations, and the countless propositions for clock escapements, Graham's dead beat, shown in elevation by Fig. 1, is at present unrivalled, except for turret clocks. A shows the last wheel in the train, which is the escape wheel, striving by the force transmitted from the weight or spring constituting the driving power, to turn in the direction of the arrow; but for the present it is stopped by the tooth B resting on what is known as the dead face of the pallet C. This, as well as the corresponding dead face on the opposite pallet D, is traced from the centre of motion of the pallets at E, so that as the pallets rock to and fro, the wheel remains stationary so long as the tooth remains on the dead face. The vibrating or rocking motion of the pallet corresponds to the vibrations of the pendulum,

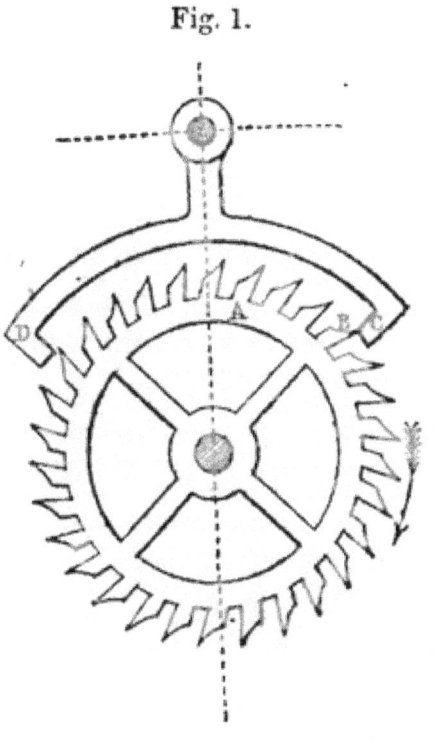

Graham's Dead-beat Escapement for Clocks.

as the crutch which engages the pendulum rod is fixed to the pallets' axis. It will be observed, that if the pallets are moved sufficiently on one side to allow the tooth to leave the dead face, it will be bearing on an inclined plane, which is called the impulse face; and it is the pressure of the tooth, as it slides over this face, that gives the little force necessary to keep the pendulum in motion. When the tooth has arrived at the end of the impulse face, and the escape wheel appears free to turn on its axis, the dead face of the pallet D is just in a position to catch the advancing tooth, and so for every two vibrations of the pendulum the escape wheel goes forward only one tooth. In the finest clocks the pallets are now jewelled, that is, made of hard stone to diminish friction and wear.

Towards the close of the seventeenth century, the science of horology had so far advanced, and mechanical appliances so much improved, that clocks were made to perform with remarkable precision, provided they were kept at a constant temperature. But the errors, when subjected to constant changes of temperature, were so perplexing to astronomers, that scientific men turned their attention to devising means to keep the effective length of the pendulum constant. Graham conceived and carried into practice, about 1715, the idea of making a jar of mercury form the pendulum bob, the height of the mercury in the jar being such, that whatever amount the pendulum rod lengthened through increase of temperature, the mercury expanded upward exactly sufficient to compensate and ensure the distance between the point of suspension and the centre of oscillation remaining constant. Many other methods of attaining the same end were invented. John Harrison (of whom more will be said in connection with the improvement of chronometers), a few years after Graham perfected the mercurial pendulum, invented a gridiron pendulum, composed of brass and iron rods, arranged so that, as the pendulum rod of iron lengthened, rods of brass on either side expanded upward. From the top of the brass rods depended other iron rods, to which the bob was suspended, the superior expansibility of the brass allowing the gridiron to be kept so short as not to interfere with the suspension of the pendulum. This ingenious device of Harrison has been many times varied by using different metals, but Graham's simple mercurial pendulum obtained the more permanent reputation, being still used as he left it, in the best regulators, with but one rival for simplicity and time-keeping qualities, viz. the system of steel and zinc compensation, used by Sir Edmund Beckett in the Westminster clock.

Till very recently, no attempt to rival the dead-beat escapement for clocks had met with success, for in fact its accuracy in clocks of reasonable size, not exposed to the weather, left nothing to be desired. The description of its action already given, shows that whatever weight was used to move the hands, was communicated through the escape wheel to the pallets, pressing upon the dead faces when the train is at rest. It will be evident, that in turret clocks, where the hands are exposed to the wind, snow, and other retarding influences, the weight being sufficient to carry the hands round under the most adverse circumstances, on some occasions when the opposing forces were at a minimum there would be much superfluous power in the train, causing the escape wheel upon leaving the dead face to press upon the impulse plane with far greater force than when the opposing forces were at a maximum.

To meet this difficulty clockmakers were in the habit of using a remontoire for turret clocks, an arrangement by which the train, instead of acting so directly on the pendulum, wound up an auxiliary power to propel it. Notwithstanding remontoires and fancy escapements occasionally used, clockmakers never expected turret clocks of any size to keep as good time as ordinary regulators, so that when the specification for making the clock for the new Houses of Parliament, drawn up by the Astronomer Royal and Mr. E. B. Denison (now Sir Edmund Beckett), stipulated that the clock should not vary more than a minute a week, most of the chief clockmakers refused to accept the stipulation, and, backed up by the Clockmakers Company, denounced it to the government as impracticable. Eventually the contract for the clock was given to Mr. Dent, Mr. Denison undertaking to design the escapement.

The idea of allowing a constant weight to fall or press upon the pendulum rod to give the required impulse had been adopted by Mudge, if it had not been accepted even before his time, but, although often elaborated with considerable ingenuity, it had never been applied so as to be absolutely reliable, until

Mr. Denison applied the gravity escapement, shown in Fig. 2, to the Westminster clock, with the astonishing result that instead of the error of the clock exceeding the stipulated one minute a week, it is reported by the Astronomer Royal to be less than one second a week.

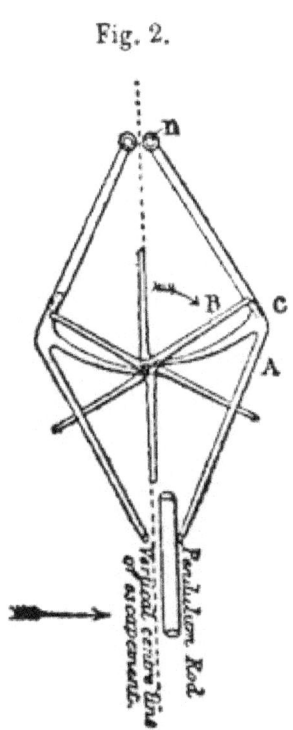

Fig. 2.

Denison's Double Three-legged Gravity Escapement.

The escape wheel, in shape something like a double Manx crest, has, near the centre, three pins which lift the pallets, but not to their extreme position. The pendulum rod, moving in the direction of the arrow, will have to lift the pallet A (which hangs freely upon the pin D) from the point where it was left by the lifting pin far enough to allow the leg or tooth B of the escape wheel to escape from the stop C; and, on its return journey, the pendulum is assisted by the falling of the pallet, not only the distance it was raised by the pendulum rod, but the amount lifted by the lifting pin also; and although the pendulum weighs 700 lbs., a pallet weighing 2 oz., lifted 1 inch in height, is sufficient to keep it going. There are many other excellent points in the Westminster clock, besides its unique escapement, which deserve noting. The pendulum bob is of adequate weight. The heavy cast-iron bracket from which the pendulum is suspended takes a firm hold of the wall of the clock room, is of a good shape for ensuring rigidity, and yet projects far enough from the wall to allow the escapement to be easily got at. The going and striking trains are well arranged on a couple of cast-iron girders upon a firm foundation. There are several original and good points connected with the striking arrangement, notably a contrivance for letting off the hammer for striking the hours within a second of true time, rendered necessary by another clause of the specification. Space will not permit a description of this ingenious device, to do justice to which many engravings would be necessary.

Countless experiments have been made with a view to the employment of electricity as a motive force for clocks. It is difficult to see what is to be gained by substituting electricity for the winding up of a weight, which seems to have been the sole aim of many inventors. Mr. R. L. Jones, the station-master at Chester, in 1857, turned electricity to good account for controlling clocks, but not for driving them. At no very remote day, a method by which clocks may be controlled will doubtless be considered a *sine quâ non*, so that the subject is therefore one of interest and not out of place.

In all systems for distributing the time, one clock— the distributor, we may call it—must be watched and corrected from observations. A clock in the Royal Observatory, Greenwich, distributes the time to a clock at the Post Office, Lombard Street, and to one at the factory of Messrs. De La Rue and Co., in Bunhill Row, before mentioned, by Jones' plan, which is simply this: The pendulum rod of the Observatory clock, in its vibrations, presses together two very weak springs, thus completing a galvanic circuit and allowing a galvanic current of opposite kinds to be transmitted at successive seconds to the clocks to be controlled, each of which has its pendulum bob composed of a hollow coil of wire. The wires from the coil pass up the pendulum rod and are led away to the controlling or distributing clock, however distant it may be. Two permanent bar magnets, having similar poles in proximity, are fixed inside the case of each controlled clock, so that the hollow coil forming the pendulum bob in its vibration passes on to and encircles each magnet alternately. The action of the currents will be to retard the vibrations of the controlled clocks, if they are going too fast, and to accelerate them, if too slow. The controlling clock is exactly of the ordinary kind, and the others differ only in having the pendulum composed of the wire coil. The clocks being reasonably good themselves, it matters not if the current fail occasionally. As long as the accumulated error is less than one beat of the pendulum, when the current is resumed it will again correct the error.

There is a system of magnetic clocks with many advantages, the invention of the late Sir Charles Wheatstone, made at the British Telegraph Manufactory, and at work at the London University, the Royal Institution, and other places. A single motor clock upon this principle will actuate sixty or seventy indicating clocks, the maintaining power being supplied by magneto-electric currents developed in a coil of wire forming the pendulum bob of the motor clock, which is made to oscillate over the poles of permanent magnets. Each indicating clock is actuated by an astatic system of magnetic needles, kept in continued rotation by these currents. The motion of these needles is communicated through a suitable train to the hands. In this way the whole circuit remains unbroken, and the currents are alternately inverted without any breaking and re-making of contacts, which is the chief source of failure in the many attempts to drive clocks by electricity.

Mr. F. Ritchie, of Edinburgh, has lately introduced an electric system of clocks, in which the pendulum is made to actuate the escapement. It seems to answer well, but it would be premature to pass a decided opinion on its merits.

The manufacture of clocks is scattered throughout the country, so that it is impossible to estimate its extent with any accuracy. The largest and most complete clock factory in England is that of Messrs. Gillett and Bland, at Croydon. They have steam power, and employ seventy or eighty workpeople; but I believe their attention is chiefly directed to large clocks.

There can be no doubt that the accurate performance of the Westminster clock, while stimulating turret clockmakers to greater excellence, has caused a demand in the colonies and foreign countries for English clocks of the larger kind. Clocks, such as are used at railway stations, made simply and cheaply, now find a market abroad. Mr. R. Webster, some years ago, drew attention to the need of improvement in the construction of railway clocks, advocating the more general adoption of a weight instead of a spring for maintaining power, and a simple kind of compensation pendulum, composed of a straight piece of seasoned deal well varnished for the rod, passing through and supporting from the bottom a hollow cylinder of zinc or lead which forms the bob; the height of the bob being sufficient to counteract the very small downward expansion of the wooden rod. Clocks of this kind keep admirable time, and are well adapted for halls and kitchens.

The manufacture of drawing-room clocks (in many instances the clock is quite subsidiary to the case) is almost entirely in the hands of the French, who turn out some very good, and also the worst, clocks that are made.

Really excellent hall clocks, in ornamental cases, are made in London. The old English eight-day clocks are still made in the rural districts, and, with heavier pendulums, would compare very favourably with most of the imported clocks. It must be admitted that there is a great want of system in the manufacture of the ordinary run of small clocks in England. A clock is a sufficiently large machine to allow of the introduction of duplicating machinery for most of the parts. The American clocks, which used to be fairly made, have sadly degenerated of late years; the cheap French clocks are wretchedly bad. It is therefore difficult to understand why English enterprise has not attempted to supply so clear a want as a cheap, plain, moderately well-made clock.

Watches and Chronometers.

Weights suspended by ropes or cords being clearly inadmissible as motive power for portable timekeepers, some other means had to be devised for driving the train, before pocket watches could be made, and about the year 1500 the mainspring is said to have been invented by Peter Hele, a clockmaker of Nuremberg. It is believed that the earliest watches were known as Nuremberg eggs. They had wheels of steel, De Wick's escapement, and an hour hand only. The early watchmakers must have found the varying force of the mainspring a source of perplexity, since several contrivances were arranged for overcoming the difficulty with more or less of success and complication, until the fusee was invented sometime between 1520 and 1530. Nothing has superseded the mainspring for driving the trains of watches, nor the fusee for equalizing the force transmitted, and both are now so well known as to require but slight description. One end of a thin ribbon of steel, called the mainspring, being fixed, the other end is wound round and round, an operation which needs increasing force as it is continued. In uncoiling, the mainspring does not expend its force directly upon the train, as the connection between the spring and the train is through the medium of a cord wound round a grooved wheel, which approaches in shape to a truncated cone, and this is called the fusee. The outline of the fusee is, or should be, in every watch, exactly proportioned to the varying force of the spring. When the spring is nearly uncoiled, or at its weakest, the cord pulls the train round with the advantage of the largest diameter of the fusee; and when the spring is fully wound, or at its strongest, it has to overcome the resistance of the train, with the cord passing over the smallest diameter of the fusee. The cord in the earlier watches was of catgut, but in 1665 a chain was introduced by Gruet, of Geneva, as a means of communication between the barrel which enclosed the mainspring and the fusee.

In 1632 Charles I. (as I have before stated) granted a charter to the clockmakers of the city of London, and at that time it may be fairly inferred, that watchmaking as well as clockmaking was flourishing as a British industry. There is, indeed, reason to suppose that the improvement of watches especially then engaged the attention of many skilful and clever Englishmen. Dr. Robert Hooke, who has already been mentioned as the inventor of a clock escapement, did as much towards perfecting timekeepers as James Watt at a later period did for the steam engine, and appears to have been one of those remarkable and versatile geniuses, before whom all difficulties fall. He, in 1658, discovered the particular suitability of a coiled spring for controlling the vibrations of watch balances. This invention of the balance spring opened the way for many minor improvements, which followed in quick succession. Thomas Tompion, often called the father of English watchmaking, by his skill no doubt assisted Hooke to demonstrate the success of his invention. Tompion and other celebrated watchmakers of the time devoted considerable attention to the construction of repeating watches.

As repeating mechanism certainly does not add to the timekeeping qualities of watches, and as, whatever the necessity for repeating watches in the seventeenth and eighteenth centuries, they can now be regarded only as toys, we need not consider them further, particularly as no repeating work whatever is now made in England. In the rare instances where English watches are furnished with repeating work, it is usually imported from Switzerland.

One consequence of the better timekeeping qualities of watches, owing to the introduction of the balance spring, was the addition of the minute hand, by Daniel Quare about 1690, and shortly after Facio, a native of Geneva, came to London and introduced the practice of jewelling, as it is called, that is making some of the rubbing surfaces of hard stone; diamonds, rubies, and sapphires being used for that purpose in the better kind, and garnet in the commoner class of watches.

In the beginning of the eighteenth century, watches were still far from being accurate timekeepers, and the possibility of solving the problem of ascertaining longitude at sea by their means, engaged the attention of many. Among them, John Harrison, a Lancashire carpenter, after a life spent in attaining his object, eventually received from the English Government in 1767 the prize of 20,000*l*., which had been offered for the invention of some means whereby it could be ascertained within 30 miles. The timekeeper with which Harrison won the prize is preserved in Greenwich

Observatory. It has a verge escapement, and resembles in shape a large silver watch. While Harrison was devoting his life to the construction of his timekeeper, others had not been idle. In 1700, George Graham, an apprentice of Tompion, invented the cylinder escapement—or, as some say, perfected it—the invention being Tompion's. The cylinder was unquestionably a great stride in advance of the verge. It is very similar in principle to the dead-beat escapement already described as invented by Graham for clocks. The pallets, however, embrace but one tooth of the escape wheel, and are formed from a cylinder which gives the title to the escapement. In spite of its superiority, it took the place of the verge escapement but slowly, and cannot be said to have entirely superseded it at any time as far as the English work is concerned. Many manufacturers who turned their attention to the cylinder escapement, abandoned it, because the cylinders were so rapidly cut away by the escape-wheel teeth, which even Mudge found a source of annoyance. He often made the cylinder of ruby, to avoid the cutting, which seemed unavoidable with brass or gold escape wheels and steel cylinders. The cylinder escapement just suited the requirements of the Swiss, who made the escape wheels of steel, with which the steel cylinders worked very well; and as this escapement allows watches to be made thin or flat, as it is called, the Swiss developed their trade with great rapidity, by making cheap watches of graceful outline.

It is remarkable that the lever escapement, invented by Thomas Mudge, about 1750, which has proved to be the best and most reliable for pocket watches, was allowed to lie by for several years. Even Mudge seems to have dismissed it from his mind, as unlikely to give the desired result, and to have turned his attention to the improvements of the verge and cylinder escapements. In 1794, Peter Litherland obtained a patent for what was called a rack lever, and a business was established at Liverpool for making watches with this escapement. The venture was a success commercially, considerable enterprise characterizing the operations of those who took up Litherland's patent. But the rack lever was not superior to the cylinder, for while Mudge and his contemporaries saw the necessity of allowing the vibrations of the balance to be as free as possible in the rack lever, the balance is never detached from the train. But the lever was evidently the right idea; and a few years after Litherland ob-

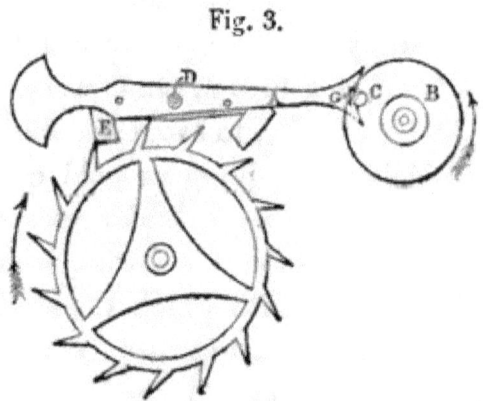

Fig. 3.

tained his patent, George Savage, by combining excellent work with proper proportion, proved its value. Fig. 3 shows the lever escapement in its ordinary form in plan, and Fig. 4 in elevation.

It will be observed that the wheel and pallet action is closely analogous to the dead-beat escapement for clocks previously described. There is one point of difference; the part of the pallet against which the

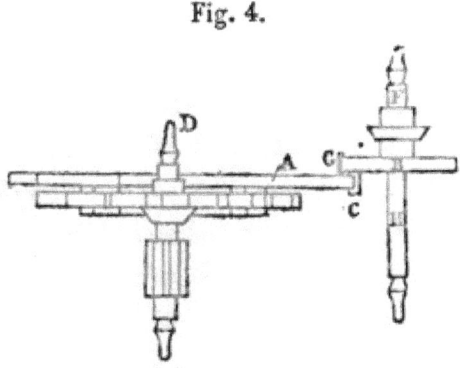

Fig. 4.

Lever Escapement.

tooth of the escape wheel is resting, instead of being in the form of a curve struck from the centre of motion of the pallets, is straight, and shaped so as to cause a slight recoil in the wheel when leaving it, with the object of preventing the pallet from being shaken out of the wheel, as would be likely to ensue, were the pallets left in the proper theoretical shape. That part of the wheel tooth in contact is also made to diverge from the radial line with the same object. Attached to the pallets and moving from the same centre is the lever (A). The roller (B) is fixed to the same arbor or staff as the balance, and revolves with it, and the only connection between the balance and the train is by means of the impulse pin (C) projecting from the roller (B). This impulse pin will be seen to be just falling into the notch of the lever, and as the balance by its impetus continues travelling in the direction of the arrow, the impulse pin, pressing upon the notch, will cause the lever and pallets to turn upon their axis (D). The impulse planes (E) of the pallet will shortly be exposed to the action of the wheel-tooth, and the opposite side of the lever notch to that which is shown as bearing on the impulse pin, will be driven against it. The force thus administered to the impulse pin is sufficient to send the balance on its vibration against the force of the balance spring, one end of which is fixed to the balance arbor at F, until the resistance of the spring, overcoming the *vis viva* of the balance, the motion of the balance is reversed, and it starts on its vibration in the opposite direction, unlocking another tooth of the wheel, and receiving another blow from the impulse pin on its way. The length of lever and diameter of roller are so arranged, that the line of contact between them is only about 30° of the roller, so that if the balance vibrates say 250° each way, 220° would be traversed quite free from any connection with the train, the balance being left more completely to the control of the spring; and in this freedom of vibration lies the great advantage of the lever over the cylinder and other preceding escapements. A small pin (G) may be observed sticking up from the lever, which prevents the pallets unlocking or leaving the wheel, except when the impulse pin is in the notch; a crescent cut from the roller allows it then to intersect the circle described by the roller edge. At other times, should a shake or blow tend to release the wheel, this safety pin would fall against the roller and prevent the pallet leaving the wheel. This safety action is made more secure in the best watches by placing a separate and smaller roller for its use on the arbor, somewhere about H; and then, instead of the pin G above the lever, there is a finger projecting from its under side to meet the roller, the smaller roller allowing a greater intersection for any given number of degrees, as any mathematician will understand. George Savage, who has been already mentioned as bringing the lever escapement to great perfection, tried several modifications in the arrangement of the means for unlocking the wheel and giving impulse to the balance, but no one of them has come into general use.

Directly Harrison placed beyond doubt the possibility of making timekeepers of sufficient accuracy to be of use to navigators, many others turned their attention to the subject and endeavoured to produce an instrument to be even more reliable than his, among them Mudge, who, although he succeeded in producing a chronometer which, upon trial, performed with more accuracy than Harrison's, left it for Arnold and Earnshaw to earn the honour of devising an escapement which should remain to the present day without improvement. Earnshaw's escapement, now generally used for marine chronometers, is admitted to be superior to Arnold's, in the points where they differed. It is shown in plan by Fig. 5 and in elevation by Fig. 6.

Its action is as follows: suppose, as in the case of

the lever escapement just noticed, that the balance, which would be fixed to the same arbor as the roller at A, is travelling in the direction of the arrow, shown

Fig. 5.

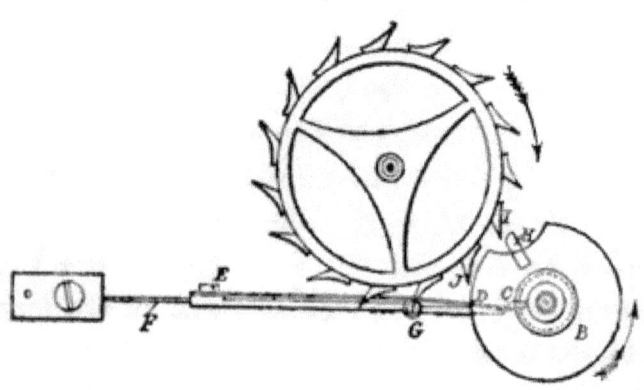

Fig. 6.

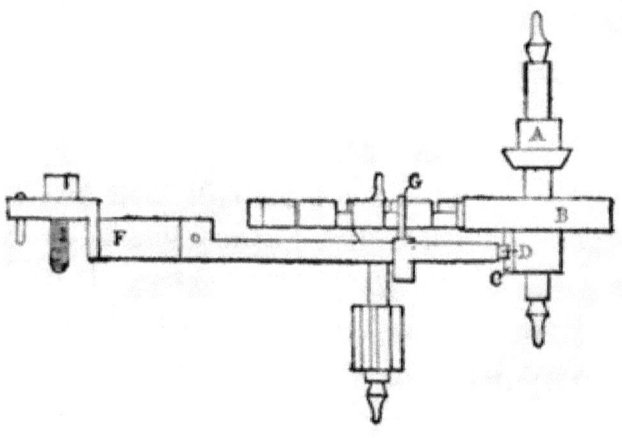

Chronometer Escapement.

in Fig. 5, close to the roller B; a projecting nib (C) in a smaller roller will catch on a long spring (D), which is fastened at one end by a screw (E). At the other end it is supported by the end of what is called the *detent.* As the nib continues to press upon the spring, the detent will bend at F and allow the tooth of the wheel, which is now bearing against the pin G, to escape; but, in the meantime, the impulse pallet (H) has passed in front of the tooth I, and by intersecting its path receives from it the necessary impulse. Directly the spring D is released by the nib, the detent flies back in time to catch the next tooth (J), and the balance continues its vibration until it is caught by the balance spring, as in the case of the lever escapement; but on the return vibration, when the nib catches the spring D, it, being no longer supported by the detent, bends towards the wheel and allows the nib to pass. The unlocking and impulse occurring only at every alternate vibration, this escapement is even more fully detached than the lever, and for a time it was thought that the spring detent or chronometer escapement would be the best also for pocket watches; but experience has shown that the shaking and jolting to which all pocket watches are more or less liable, render the lever preferable. The same delicacy of action prevented the duplex, which may be considered theoretically a superior escapement to the lever, obtaining that hold upon public favour which it was expected to do thirty or forty years ago.

The fact that changes of temperature cause a variation in the strength of balance springs, was of little consequence in the time of Dr. Hooke in the presence of much greater errors, the result of imperfect escapements and comparatively rough work; but Harrison found it necessary to endeavour to compensate this variation, by applying what he called a curb to the spring, so as to keep its effect on the balance uniform. Earnshaw preferred to compensate for the variation of the length and elasticity of the spring, in the balance, the rim of which he made of brass and steel soldered together with the brass outside. Since Earnshaw's time there has been a general disinclination to interfere with the free action of the spring, and the compensation balance shown in Fig. 7, which is substantially that of Earnshaw, is in very general use for marine chro-

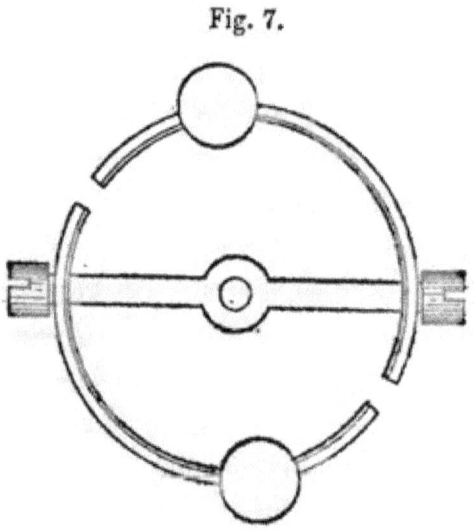

Fig. 7.

Ordinary Compensation Balance.

nometers and for pocket watches of the best class, with the exception that for watches, a number of screws with heavy heads are substituted for the two weights as shown.

The Astronomer Royal (Sir G. B. Airy) has demonstrated by experiment the fact, that the alteration in the force of the balance spring varies in the same ratio as the temperature, and the movement of the weights to or from the centre of the balance is about in the same proportion. But as the *vis viva* or controlling power of a balance varies in the same proportion as the square of its diameter, the compensation will be hardly perfect. Not a little ingenuity has been expended during the last thirty or forty years, in endeavouring to contrive something better than the ordinary compensation balance; most of the attempts being in the direction of auxiliaries, as they are called, or the application of something to assist the ordinary balance. Of late years Kullberg's flat-rim balance, without an auxiliary, has attracted considerable attention, from the successful performance of marine chronometers fitted with it.

This endeavour to achieve perfection is encouraged by the annual competitive trials of marine chronometers which take place at Greenwich Observatory, under the superintendence of the Astronomer Royal; and there is no doubt that to these trials is due, to a great extent, the fact that England now monopolizes the chronometer making of the world. Instead of being cased like a watch, as Harrison's chronometer was, the practice has become usual of suspending the marine chronometer upon gymbals, similar to the manner in which a millstone is hung, so that it may be as far as possible free from the motion of the ship. The gymbal ring is fixed to the inside of a wooden box about 7 inches square, which encloses the chronometer. The whole is placed in a still larger box, which is padded to keep the temperature as uniform as possible. With the exception of an insignificant number produced in Liverpool, the marine chronometer trade is confined to London, where about 1500 are manufactured yearly. The movements are made in Lancashire, and the manufacturing divided into branches in much the same way as watchmaking, which will be described presently.

When the Clockmakers' Company was incorporated in 1632, the city of London was doubtless the centre of British clock and watchmaking. But with the subdivision of labour induced by the demand for English timekeepers, Clerkenwell became the head-quarters of artificers in the various branches, and maintained pre-eminence in every branch of watchmaking, as long as verge watches held the field. With the introduction of the lever escapement, the movement making, which comprises the barrel, fusee, the two plates which hold the train together, and the wheels and pinions, migrated to Lancashire. It will readily be understood that in the eighteenth century, although the production of the different parts of a watch had been subdivided as much as possible, yet where any other than pure hand labour was used, the mechanical aids were of the rudest kind, and there was no particular standard of size either for the completed watch or for the different parts; each manufacturer starting with his own idea of what would be the most perfect proportion and the most acceptable size. When the movement making became transferred to Lancashire, the same want of system and consequent waste prevailed. And no real advance towards uniformity was made, until Mr. Wycherley, of Prescot, in 1866, introduced his system of machine-made movements. Mr. Wycherley adopted eight standard sizes for movements, the smallest 1·34 inch diameter and the largest 1·83 inch diameter. He built a factory and erected steam machinery of such a character, that the different parts for thousands of movements are made perfectly interchangeable, the machinery for some of the processes being attended by girls. In addition to Mr. Wycherley's factory at Prescot, watch movements are made on a smaller scale at other places in the Prescot district, which includes St. Helens, Rainhill, Cronton, and Widnes, the total production of the district being now estimated at from 100,000 to 120,000 movements yearly. Movements are also made to a small extent in Coventry. Besides the movements, some of the watch-hands are made in Lancashire, the remainder of the branches being conducted at the manufacturing centres, which are Clerkenwell, Coventry, Liverpool, and Birmingham.

After the movement comes into the hands of the manufacturer, it is usually sent first to the dial-maker, who makes a suitable dial.

In the making of watch dials, several distinct trades are included. White enamel dials with black figures painted thereon are the most generally used and have a nice effect, but, however truly divided, are liable to distortion in firing. Gold and silver dials retain their accuracy of division and admit of considerable elaboration.

What may really be termed the heart of the watch—

the escapement—is divided into two or three branches; the wheel-cutter cuts the escape wheel, the pallet-maker makes the pallets to suit the wheel, the escapement-maker makes the lever and roller and the arbors connected therewith, which may be seen on referring to the drawing of the lever escapement. Having marked off the proper positions for the pivots upon the plates, he sends them to the jeweller to jewel the holes. Then the finisher arranges the proper depths of the train, and sends the plates once more to the jeweller, to have the jewels fixed into such holes as may have been decided on. The fusee has to be cut by the fusee-cutter, and then the finisher applies the chain to connect the barrel and fusee, and fixes the mainspring in the barrel, so that the pull upon the train through the fusee is uniform, however much or little the mainspring is wound. The stopwork has to be finished, and if the watch is to be keyless, the keyless-work fitted. The case-maker, balance-maker, and hand-maker, having contributed their work, the examiner fits the movement to the case and puts on the hands. Then comes the most artistic performance. The balance spring has to be applied, so that the vibrations of the balance all occupy the same time, irrespective of the number of degrees travelled through. The greatest delicacy and skill are required in curving the ends of the spring. A watch of the finest kind would have the outer coil of the spring curved into the centre, after the manner introduced by Breguet, a celebrated French watchmaker, and would have no index nor curb pins to alter the length of the spring.

The screws of the balance would be adjusted with the utmost care, so that the watch could keep time at temperatures of between 40° and 90°. For this purpose are used an ice-box and an oven, which latter is a sheet-iron chamber heated by jets of gas. The ability to dispense with the index shows a grand stride in watch-making.

While English watchmakers have aimed at perfection and reliability in their productions, the Swiss, and latterly the Americans, have turned their attention more particularly to decreasing the cost of manufacture. The Swiss introduced what is called the going barrel, dispensing with the chain and fusee, and allowing the varying force of the mainspring to be transmitted to the escapement. The going barrel has many champions, but as it is clear that the mainspring, when unwound, must be strong enough to drive the escapement, when it is fully wound, a great waste of power occurs in one of the smallest and most delicate machines where economy of power is greatly to be desired. The going barrel is never used for the best English work, and English watchmakers are often reproached for their blindness to its merits, but perhaps the best evidence of the unsatisfactory nature of the going barrel is, the many endeavours to make its action more analogous to the fusee.

The demand for keyless watches has no doubt caused the freer introduction of the going barrel into English work, as the keyless mechanism is more easily applied with the going barrel than with the fusee. The idea of stem-winding is not new, for Earnshaw's contemporary,

Arnold, made watches to wind from the pendant, but without arrangement for setting the hands in that way. In first-rate watches the ability to set the hands without a key is almost needless, and the facility of winding without a key is dearly purchased at the cost of the fusee. Mr. Kullberg has introduced one of the best methods of keyless-winding work for fusee watches with hunting cases, in which the keyless work is quite out of action unless the case is opened.

All watch-cases made in the United Kingdom must, by legislative enactment, be assayed and marked with the government stamp, and the number of cases marked will therefore afford some indication of the state of the watch trade, although it will not be an exact criterion, as foreign watches and watches partly of foreign make, are occasionally put into English cases. The greater part are marked at the Goldsmith's Hall, London. Of the provincial halls, Chester ranks first according to the number of cases marked, and Birmingham next. In 1796 there were marked at the London Hall 6576 gold and 185,102 silver cases, a total unequalled before or since. Of this number it may be conjectured that many were for the worthless forgeries, that a few years after proved so disastrous to the English trade. In 1816, 10,766 gold and 91,346 silver cases were marked at the London Hall, and in addition to those marked in London, silver cases weighing 10,368 oz. were marked at Birmingham in 1796, and 36,692 oz. in 1816. At that time the Birmingham cases would represent nearly the Coventry trade, but many of the cases for Coventry watches are now made or marked in London. In 1848, 14,257 gold and 73,071 silver cases were marked in London, 1743 gold and 6227 silver at Chester (indicating the marked progress of the watch manufacture at Liverpool since the last return quoted), and 203 gold cases and silver cases weighing 236 oz. at Birmingham. In 1855, 20,817 gold and 90,062 silver cases were marked at the London Hall, 7011 gold and 16,336 silver at Chester, and 200 gold cases and silver cases weighing 217 oz. at Birmingham. In 1867, 25,437 gold and 98,143 silver cases were marked in London, 12,530 gold and 18,000 silver cases at Chester, and silver cases weighing 12,000 oz. at Birmingham.

The return for 1867 is the last official statement issued, but I have ascertained that there has been a steady increase since that time, and that during the year ended the 29th of May, 1874, there were marked at the Goldsmith's Hall, London, 31,275 gold and 109,814 silver cases, in all 141,089 cases, and during the year ended 29th of May, 1875, 32,888 gold and 112,323 silver, or 145,211 cases altogether, being the largest number marked there in a similar period for many years.

Until the United States adopted their present prohibitive import duties, a very large number of uncased watches were sent there from Liverpool, the Americans making the cases themselves, and in many instances imitating the English Hall marks, which in the absence of any law regulating the marking of watch cases, they were enabled to do without concealment.

The number of uncased watches exported now is

very small, and would not more than counterbalance the movements of Swiss manufacture which are fitted to English cases.

Taking the number of cases marked as an indication, it is clear that the English watch trade is making progress, although the advance is not so rapid as might have been expected in a country pre-eminent for mechanical genius. The American system of manufacturing watches has been much vaunted, but such a method of wholesale manufacture appears quite unsuited to the finer class of work for which England holds the markets of the world.

MUSICAL INSTRUMENTS.

By E. F. RIMBAULT, LL.D. (Musical Examiner, College of Preceptors).

In giving an account of some of the most important improvements that have taken place in the manufacture of musical instruments, I have arranged the material under these heads: 1, the Organ; 2, the Pianoforte; 3, Free-Reed Instruments; 4, Wind Instruments of Wood; 5, Wind Instruments of Brass. This classification does not include instruments played with a bow, such as the violin, violoncello, &c., as in all essential particulars they remain the same as when first invented. The harp, guitar, &c., are still under manufacture, but in such small numbers as almost to predict their final extinction, a result which has taken place with so many instruments of the lute tribe. For this reason they are not represented in this article.

Makers of musical instruments have increased in Great Britain since 1861, though not to the extent that might have been anticipated, as even now they only number about 8000 males, a small number when we take into consideration the progress of music during the last ten years. This may be accounted for by the large number of instruments imported from France and Germany. Indeed, from the Report of the Commissioners of Her Majesty's Customs, we learn that the annual value of those imported from France alone is nearly 300,000*l*. This will explain the comparatively small extent of our English manufacture.

The Organ.

It is seriously to be regretted that the early history of this instrument, the largest, the most majestic, and the richest in its variety of effects, should be involved in doubt and obscurity. Such, however, is the fact; indeed the period of its invention is unknown, whilst fiction and conjecture have in this, as in similar cases, usurped the place of probability and truth.

This has arisen chiefly from the enlarged sense in which the Latin word *organum* has been used. Originally it had a very extended meaning, and answered to almost every kind of implement, for whatever purpose employed: by degrees it became confined to instruments of music generally, afterwards to those in which wind was employed, and finally to the single instrument which still bears its name.

Passing by all conjecture, this much is certain, that the organ is very ancient, and, however degrading, we must submit to the conclusion that the syrinx, or "Pipe of Pan," composed of several reeds joined together, and the bagpipe, are the humble progenitors of the stately instrument with which we are acquainted at the present day. The hydraulic organ, said to have been invented by Ctesibius, of Alexandria (B.C. 120), was extensively used by the Greeks and Romans, who employed it both privately and in their theatres and temples. Though the exact nature and construction of this instrument are unknown, some little information concerning it may be gleaned from the works of Hero of Alexandria, and of Vitruvius, from which it appears that it corresponded with our present idea of an organ in many essential particulars. In 757, the Emperor Constantine V. sent an organ to King Pepin, which was placed in the church of St. Cornelius at Compiègne. In 812, Louis-le-Débonnaire placed one in the church of Aix-la-Chapelle, and one is mentioned as existing in the church of Winchester in the tenth century. These instruments had no keyboard, and the wind was let into the pipes by drawing back a rod or lever. In the first keyboard the keys were very large, and were struck by the fist; but in the twelfth century an improvement was made in this respect, and the use of compound stops, and the introduction of pedals, opened a new era in the history of the instrument. A gradual course of improvement is traced in organs erected at Dijon, in the thirteenth century; at Halberstadt, in 1360; and at Nuremberg in 1468, about which period pipes of the large dimensions of 16 and 32 feet began to be made. The description handed down to us of organs erected in the latter part of the following century, proves that at that date, all the principal stops now employed had come into use, and, to quote the words of Professor Pole, " that the general plan of a large organ in all its most important particulars, had arrived at the point at which it now stands, the only further progress made since, having been in the mechanical details of the construction."

The organ is composed of several ranges of pipes, some of which are of wood, or a mixture of tin and lead, with open mouths like the flute played at the end, and the rest of which have in their mouthpiece, tongues of brass, or reeds. These pipes are placed upright upon the end in which their mouthpiece is, in holes which are made in the upper part of certain wooden boxes called wind-chests. Large bellows distribute the wind into tubes which communicate with the interior of the wind-chests. To each range of pipes is attached a plate or rod of wood, which is also pierced with holes at distances equal to those of the wind-chest. This plate or rod is called the register. It is arranged in such a manner as to move easily when it is drawn out or pushed in by the organist. If the register is pushed in, its holes do not correspond to those of the wind-chest in which the pipes are placed, and consequently the wind cannot enter into the pipes, but if it is drawn out, the holes will perfectly correspond, and the air may be admitted into the pipes. Then, when the organist places his finger upon a key, the latter, as it sinks down, draws a little rod which opens a valve corresponding to the hole in the register, the wind enters, and the pipe of the note gives the sound which belongs to that note. If several registers are drawn out, all the pipes in them which correspond to the note touched will sound at the same time. If the pipe is a flute, the sound is produced by the vibration of the column of air in the pipe; if it is a reed-stop, the sound results from the beating of the tongue, which breaks the air against the walls of the mouth of the pipe.

Besides the variety of sounds which arise from this difference of principle in their production, the organ has others, which are the result of the different forms and sizes of the pipes. Without going further into this part of the subject, which would lead us far away from the object before us, I may briefly remark that some pipes are terminated by smaller pipes called *chimneys;* others have the form of two inverted cones placed upon one another; others are in the shape of long cylinders; so that each has its peculiar quality of sound. When a series of pipes of the same quality of tone are used collectively, it is called a *stop*. The modern inventions in this respect are very few. The *Keraulaphon* was invented by Messrs. Gray and Davison, and first introduced by them in the organ of St. Paul's, Wilton Place. This is an 8-feet manual stop, generally ending at tenor C. The pipes of metal have a hole bored in them near the top which gives them a peculiar quality of tone, something like the *Dulciana*, but less subdued, as it is of larger scale. The *Tuba-Mirabilis*, invented by the late Mr. Hill, is an 8-feet reed stop—the most powerful reed made. It has a separate bellows and wind-chest, with a pressure of 11 inches, the ordinary pressure for church organs being from $2\frac{1}{2}$ to 3 inches. The pipes generally project nearly horizontally from the top of the instrument. Its effect is very grand. The *Flute-Harmonique* (invented by the celebrated Cavaillé Coll, of Paris), is an application of a peculiar phenomenon of sound worth attention. Everyone knows that a flute or similar instrument, if blown with undue strength, sounds an octave above the true note;

the false note, however, from the increased pressure of wind, being more powerful. This principle is applied in the case before us. The pipes of the *flute-harmonique* are "overblown," and made to sound their octaves. This phenomenon may be called the reverse of that of stopped pipes. In the latter case an 8-feet pipe sounds only a 4-feet note, the one, however, being a soft, suppressed sound, the other powerful and clear. This stop is found generally in very large organs only, or on a solo organ, with separate wind reservoir and keyboard, together with the *tuba-mirabilis*, and other solo stops. The *Harmonic Diapason*, a 16-feet diapason, sounds the same notes as one of 8 feet, but with a power that is magnificent. By sufficiently increasing the pressure of wind, even the second octave may be produced. Thus it will be seen that by stopping on the one hand, and overblowing on the other, a pipe of given length may be made to speak in no less than four different octaves. The *Diocton* stop, invented by Mr. Holditch, has the effect of doubling every single stop throughout the instrument, thus making it equivalent to one with twice the number of stops. The contrivance is very simple, and is applied to church and chamber organs.

There are two kinds of bellows, diagonal and horizontal. Of these the former is the older, and by far the less effective kind. Probably, in this country, few instances of the diagonal bellows would now be met with, having been generally replaced by the horizontal with great advantage; although German builders still give the preference to the former.

Attached to the middle of the bellows is a square wooden chimney called the wind-trunk, up which the wind is propelled into the wind-chest. It is a rectangular shallow box, varying in size, according to the number of pipes to be supplied from it, the latter being placed immediately over and upon it. Hanging from the roof, as it were, and extending from side to side is a row of triangular wooden pallets, the two sides of which slope off downwards, so as to present a gable end, the shape of an acute-angled triangle. The sharp edge pointing downwards offers the least possible resistance to the compressed air, when the pallet is drawn down by the key with which it is connected. There is a pallet to every key (on the clavier to which the wind-chest pertains) working on a hinge at the back, and kept up against the pallet hole by a steel wire spring. Many ingenious contrivances have been invented of late to obviate the inconvenience occasioned by the resistance of the compressed air on the pallet, which, however, do not come within my scope, nor could any description be rendered fully intelligible without diagrams. The principal of these only, called the *Pneumatic Lever*, calls for a little attention.

This most important feature in the modern organ, its purpose being to lighten the touch, is the invention of Mr. Barker. It must be borne in mind that, in putting down a key, the finger has to overcome the force exercised by the spring of the sound-board pallet to keep it closed, as well as the compressed air in the wind-chest. Very large organs have pallets of proportionate size, and commonly two in each key in the bass; also generally some stops on a "heavy wind," i. e. their wind closely compressed, so that the pipes speak very powerfully. All these causes combine to make the touch very "heavy," so as to be most fatiguing to the player. Various attempts have been made to obviate this drawback and "lighten the touch," the most successful of which is the pneumatic lever, consisting of a small box, divided crossways inside two little chambers, connected by a channel between them. In the bottom of each of these chambers is an opening, covered by a pallet. Beneath these pallets is suspended a backfall connected in the usual way, each with its respective key. From each arm of this backfall a perpendicular rod arises, and is attached to the pallet above, so that when the backfall moves on its centre, one pallet is pushed up to open, and the other is pulled down to shut. Over this box, and communicating with both the chambers, is a little bellows, like a feeder, which constitutes the pneumatic lever.

The farther chamber is a wind-chest, into which wind is forced. When the key is pressed down, the far end of the backfall rises and pushes up the pallet of the wind-chest; the wind rushes through and up the channel into the lever above, expanding it, and raising the outer end which carries on the key action; and thus it becomes a motive power to open the soundboard pallets. When the key returns to its place, the action is reversed; the pallet of the wind-chest being pulled down, cuts off the supply of wind to the lever, which thereupon collapses, and discharges its contents into the other chamber, whose pallet being open allows the wind to escape.

Another little contrivance is found in modern organs of moderate size. On the wind-trunk a small bellows is suspended. This is called a *Concussion Bellows*, and its object is to steady the wind. If the bellows is blown with an unsteady jerking action, or if the player by a rapid transition from piano to forte (i. e. throwing out, whilst playing, several stops at once by a composition pedal) make a sudden large demand upon the wind in the reservoir, the jerk will be communicated to the speech of the pipes, and produce a very disagreeable effect. This evil is remedied by the concussion bellows. When the wind is " put in," some of it makes its way through a hole in the wind-trunk into the concussion bellows, partly inflating it, and raising the upper board (i. e. moving it outwards, as it generally hangs perpendicularly). The expansion is opposed by a spring. When the pressure from the causes such as I have mentioned becomes uneven, the concussion bellows affords a means of escape for the superfluity, becoming further inflated, and the spring thereby more compressed. The moment that the wind resumes its proper pressure, the spring causes the bellows to return to its ordinary position.

A great improvement was made by the late Mr. Hill, in 1851, in the arrangement of the trunks or passages conveying the compressed air from the bellows to the wind-chests of the sound-boards. These are, in large organs, of considerable size, and, as usually placed, are inconveniently in the way of the various movements and machinery connected with the keys, stops, composition pedals, &c. They can be dispensed with altogether by making the framing and main standards, which support the sound-board, hollow, and using them as wind passages. This ingenious contrivance leaves the space under the sound-boards completely free and open, and gives increased facilities for the better arrangement of the action.

Various inventions have recently been brought into use for dispensing with manual labour in supplying the organ with wind. Gas and water engines are both employed, the most successful being Joy's Patent Hydraulic Engine, patented in 1856. A list of the organs to which this invention has been applied is given in Rimbault and Hopkins' work on 'The Organ; its History and Construction,' second edition, p. 68.

The organ now contains some mechanical contrivances which belong exclusively to the modern style of building. Among the foremost of these rank what are called *Couplers*, viz. movements by the aid of which different sets of keys may be made to act with each other, or be *coupled* together, thus gaining additional power and variety. I will take the most common manual coupler, viz. pedal to great. At the back of the keyboard may be observed (between the backs of the great and swell keys) a set of short strikers, one to each key, passing through a frame which reaches from side to side. This is connected with the draw-stop handle, which is now in, and all the strikers are lying inclosed at an angle of 45 degrees with the keys, so that if the lower row of keys be played on, they will not be interfered with. Now we pull out the draw stop, and the frame in which the strikers work is made to take a quarter turn, whereby the strikers are brought into an upright position, the bottom ends resting on the tail of the great organ keys, whilst their tops come immediately under the corresponding keys of the swell. If one of the lower keys be now touched, it pushes up the striker, which, by elevating the *back* of the key above, produces the same effect as if the *front* of it had been depressed by the player. Thus any note or notes played on the lower manual are executed on the upper. When this union is not required, the stop is pushed in, and the strikers resume their slanting position.

A very superior piece of mechanism is the *sliding coupler*, which is arranged as follows: the *upper* edge of the back-end of the keys of the *lower* manual is cut away for a few inches, leaving an inclined plane sloping backwards. In the *under* edge of the keys above is a similar incision, with the incline reversed. Through this hollow is let a tapped wire, having a regulating button at the end. Then there is a set of upright strikers in a register as before, with heads like that of a hammer. In this case, however, the register does not revolve, but *slides inwards*, on the handle being drawn. This motion causes the bottom end of the strikers to glide up the inclined plane in the lower row of keys, thus causing their heads, which, before rested on the register, to rise a little, at the same time bringing them exactly under the regulating button. In this position the stickers act as before. When the handle is pushed in, the register returns to its original place where the strikers hang over the hollow of the keys below, which can then rise without touching them.

Composition Pedals, the purpose of which is to draw out or push in certain combinations of the stops by the feet, thus saving the necessity of the hands being removed from the keys, are now found in all organs. They are said to have been invented by Mr. Bishop in 1809, but were really invented by Jordan in 1730, and improved by the latter. Of these there are two kinds, the single and the double action. The former acts in one way only, i. e. it either draws certain stops out or in, but does not do *both*. The latter kind performs both offices, and is of course much superior. In modern organs of moderate size there are usually two or three double-action composition pedals controlling the great organ stops, and probably one or two to the swell and pedals. Mr. Willis, the eminent organ builder, has patented a clever contrivance for working these pedals by a row of studs in the beading under the great organ keyboard, effected by the aid of a pneumatic apparatus on the same principle as that applied to the keys.

The most recent improvement with regard to the organ is the application of electricity and insulated wire, to replace or supersede the action. It is not merely a new process to attain the same end, but, independently of the suppression of a multitude of moving parts, many new advantages are presented otherwise unattainable. The touch is more delicate, rapid, uniform, and invariable. The durability is increased, owing to the absence of wear and tear. The keyboards can now be placed at any required distance from and quite irrespective of the relative position of the organ itself; therefore the organist may choose a position where he can hear the effects which he produces, and the voices which he leads or accompanies, without in any way increasing the complication or liability to derangement. Many positions can now be utilized with the grandest effect that were formerly utterly impracticable. Powerful west-gallery organs may be played from the east end of the church, entirely through a cable of insulated wire an inch in diameter, or attached to additional manuals provided for that purpose at a mechanical organ placed close to the choir. Any disposition of the organ, as the architectural arrangements of the building suggest themselves, is now perfectly practicable.

The perfection of the system is due to Mr. Barker (the inventor of the pneumatic action), and its application has been successfully carried out by Messrs. Bryceson and Co.

England and Germany are the only countries in which the art of organ building has been carried out with anything like care and assiduity; the artists of both countries have made various improvements, and although the English organs cannot enumerate so many stops as some of those on the continent (which augmentation consists principally of half stops and duplicates one of the other), yet in the variety and general arrangements they are found to be superior instruments.

A great boon has lately been conferred on the public by the manufacture of small organs at reasonable prices, sufficiently powerful to support a small body of singers. I may instance in particular Lewis' *Lieblich organs*. They contain a Lieblich Gedact C C to G, and an open diapason, of a full round tone, to tenor D. They are provided with feet blowers like a harmonium, and are tasteful in design—in fact, all that could be desired. Mr. Lewis' example is being followed by other makers in making "chancel organs," as they are termed.

The manufacture of organs, it will be readily understood, from the nature of the instrument and its limited demand, is a very small branch of trade. The Post-office Directory numbers only forty-two makers in London, and some of these are only pipe-makers, and men who undertake organ building upon commission. Besides these we have a few local builders, scattered through various parts of England, and one or two in Edinburgh and Dublin. These men, with few exceptions, are in a small way of business, and employed chiefly in repairing and tuning.

It is believed that the entire number of organs, large and small (a great proportion being of the latter description), annually manufactured in Great Britain, does not exceed twelve or thirteen hundred.

The Pianoforte.

The history of this instrument, together with the gradual improvements that have been made in its construction, is singularly identical with the rise and progress of modern music itself. The instrument that immediately preceded it was the harpsichord, in which the wire was twitched by a small tongue of crow-quill attached to an apparatus called a jack, moved by the key. The tone thus produced has been not inaptly described as "a scratch with a sound at the end of it." This instrument, although great ingenuity was displayed in its manufacture, was very monotonous, and afforded the player no scope except for execution, and that of a most mechanical and soulless kind. At length in an auspicious hour for the interests of music, the idea arose that by causing the key to *strike* the string instead of *pulling* it, the tone might be considerably improved, and the general capabilities of the instrument otherwise extended. This contrivance opened an entirely new field to the player, by giving him the power of expression in addition to that of execution; for by varying the touch a greater or less degree of force could be given to the blow on the string, whereby the effects of *piano* and *forte* might be produced at pleasure. This was the great feature of the new invention, and gave to the improved instrument the name of *pianoforte*, which it has ever since retained. The merit of the invention has been ascribed by turns to the Germans, Italians, French, and the English; but I think that in my 'History of the Pianoforte,' I have satisfactorily proved that the claim of priority is in favour of Bartolomeo Cristofali, of Padua, who made the first pianoforte (in reality a harpsichord with hammers) in or shortly after 1710. There can be no doubt, however, that important improvements in the instrument were subsequently made by German manufacturers, Silbermann, Stein, and others, and that to an Englishman, the Rev. W. Mason, the well-known poet, is to be ascribed the contrivance of detaching the hammer from the key, and giving it only a momentary connection when the key is struck by the finger. Mason's valuable improvement was adopted by the English makers, who became celebrated for the superiority of their pianofortes towards the close of the last century, a celebrity which they have ever since maintained. In all the cities of the civilized world, makers of this instrument arose, and a suitable style of music and school of players were not long wanting. It is needless to describe the different varieties now in use of an instrument so familiar to everyone. Our principal makers have rivalled each other in their exertions to increase the powers and improve the mechanism of their instruments; and while those of each maker have some distinguishing feature of excellence, no one can be said to have gained a general pre-eminence over the others.

The pianoforte was first introduced into England about the year 1757, at which time various German mechanics came over to work at the instrument, the most successful amongst whom was John Zumpé. The earliest pianofortes were of the square form. It was not until 1781 that John Broadwood and Robert Stodart, after many experiments, succeeded in producing the grand action, which, with slight modifications, has kept its place until the present time. Broadwood's first patent is dated July 17, 1773, and states that it is "for his new constructed pianoforte, which is far superior to any instrument of the kind hitherto made." It was principally noticeable for the position of the wrestpins and the shape of the hammers and dampers. In 1800, Muzio Clementi and Frederick Collard commenced business, and added further improvements to the mechanism of the instrument. In 1828, Robert Wornum brought out the *piccolo* action for upright cottage pianofortes; and since this date various important improvements have been added by the Messrs. Broadwood, Collard, Kirkman, Brinsmead, &c. To the late Ralph Allison is due the credit of introducing divisional labour and machinery in the construction of the several parts of the pianoforte, a system which has tended greatly to cheapen and popularize the instrument.

The division of labour in the manufacture of the pianoforte is extremely great, as each instrument, in a large firm, passes through the hands of nearly forty of the workmen. The principal divisions of manufacture are—the framing and sound-board, the stringing, the keys and machinery for striking the strings (technically called the *action*), and the ornamental case covering the whole. The latter, of course, belongs to cabinet manufacture and decorative art.

The head, or framing of a pianoforte, is a part of the utmost importance, as upon it depends the durability of the instrument, and its power of standing in tune. It is necessarily of great strength. The old instruments were strung with such light wire as not to require any great strength of frame to support the tension, but when thicker wire was employed to produce a more powerful tone, extra framing became necessary, and the use of metal bracings. One reason for the increase of strain was, that patents were granted in England for great improvements upon the soft Belgian steel wire, and the English wire could be drawn up to the pitch, which was continually being raised without danger of breaking. From these causes the tension of the strings became enormous, amounting in a three-unison full-grand pianoforte to sixteen tons. It will then be readily conceived that the strength of framing to resist this force must be considerable. I agree with Professor Pole, that the important part which iron, under the auspices of the engineering profession, began to take in the constructive arts at the commencement of the present century, had some influence upon the manufacture of the pianoforte. As early as 1808 Messrs. Broadwood applied metal tension bars to the treble; in 1820 Mr. Stodart patented the first perfect system of metallic bracing for grand instruments; and between this date and 1827, other makers applied various modifications of this system, which resulted in the general plan now in use.

" The compass of the pianoforte for a long time was only five octaves and a half. Francis Panormo, a pianist of some note, was the first to suggest the idea of extending its range, and John Broadwood and Sons were the first to try the experiment. Their first addition was half an octave of keys in the treble, to C altissimo. The scale was afterwards carried down to C C C in the bass, forming a compass of six octaves. It was then carried up to F in the treble, forming six octaves and a half; and when another note was added to G, it was called six octaves and three-quarters, although it was in reality only six and a half octaves. After this, the addition of the treble A made the compass what is called six and seven-eighths octaves; while that and the bass notes to A formed the complete seven octaves. These additions were made at different and irregular times, as the mechanical resources of the manufacturer become enlarged, and pianoforte playing progressed."

One of the greatest improvements in the pianoforte was the substitution of heavier wires. In the old pianoforte each string was formed of a separate wire, one end of which was twisted into a loop, and passed over the stud in the string block; the other end being wrapped round the wrestpin. When thicker wire was adopted, it became impossible to form the loop, and this gave rise to the modern method of stringing, according to which one wire of double length is made to form two strings. The two ends are wrapped round two adjoining wrestpins; the middle of the wire being bent over a stud in the string-plate, at the opposite end of the instrument. The pressure of the wire on the stud is sufficient to keep both strings distinct, as regards their tuning. This method of stringing was invented and patented by Messrs. Collard, in 1827, and is now almost universally adopted.

By the *action* is understood the machinery, through which the impulse given by the finger of the player is transmitted to the string of the instrument. The action is the moving part, and upon its capability to speak the will or mind of the performer depends its excellence. The earliest action was very rude. The hammer was lifted by an upright wire attached to the back-end of the key, and capped with a leather button, which came in contact with the under side of the hammer. The height of the button was so adjusted, that when the key was pressed down as far as it would go, the hammer was at a short distance from the string; the effect of this adjustment being that, after the impulse given to the hammer had caused it to strike the blow, it fell back upon the button, and so left the string free to vibrate. This was called the "single action." "It was," says Professor Pole, "the simplest form of mechanism, and probably the earliest that attained for the pianoforte any share of public favour. Square instruments were made with this action as late as the commencement of the present century, and probably many of them are in existence still." The invention of the hopper was the next great improvement. "The evil of the single action," says the authority just quoted, "was that, owing to the adjustment already mentioned, the hammer would not reach the string, unless the key was thrust down with sufficient force to give it considerable impetus, so that it was impossible to play very *piano;* while if, to remedy this evil, the adjustment of the button was altered to bring the hammer nearer to the string, there was a danger of its not leaving it after the blow, a defect technically called 'blocking.' The hopper remedied this evil. It was a jointed upright piece attached to the back-end of the key, and used to lift the hammer, in place of the stiff wire and button of the former mechanism. When the key was pressed down, the hopper, engaging in a notch on the under side of the hammer, lifted it to within a very short distance of the string; so near, in fact, that almost the slightest pressure would cause it to strike; but at this moment, while the key was still pressed down, the jointed part of the hopper coming in contact with a fixed button as it rose, escaped from, or 'hopped' out of the notch, and let the hammer fall clear away from the string. This mechanism as applied, with trifling variation, to the square pianoforte was called the 'double action,' and is extensively in use for this and the upright form at the present day."

The invention of the check remedied a defect which I shall next explain. The hammer, when liberated from the hopper, fell upon a rail covered with cloth, or some other soft bed prepared to receive it. Now, when a forcible blow was struck, there was always a danger of the hammer rebounding, or, in other words, the elasticity of the struck wire would send it down with such force that it rebounded from its bed, touched the string a second time, and so damped the vibration and injured the tone. The remedy for this was found in fixing to the back-end of the key a projection called a "check," which caught the edge of the hammer as it fell, and held it down so firmly that it could not again rise. The check was one of the most important additions ever made to the action; and no pianoforte, of any pretensions, is considered complete without it. The next invention applied to the action of the pianoforte is called the repetition mechanism, and its object

K

is thus described: "In the ordinary action, after the hammer has fallen, the key must rise to its position of rest before the hopper will engage again in the notch of the hammer, so as to be ready for another stroke; and hence a note cannot be repeated without not only requiring the finger to be lifted through the entire height of the key's motion, but also demanding a length of time between the repetitions sufficient to allow of its full rise. The contrivances by which the inconvenience has been overcome are of various kinds, according to the fancy or ingenuity of the makers; but they all act on the same principle, namely, by holding up the hammer at a certain height while the key returns; by which means the hopper is allowed to engage itself under the hammer earlier, and to reproduce the note in less time, and with less labour to the finger than before."

Although the last twenty years does not record the introduction of any very important novelty in the pianoforte, yet a considerable general advance has taken place in its manufacture. "The best class of instruments, in the hands of the first-rate makers, have improved both in quality of tone and in perfection of make; while the manufacture of instruments of a more humble description has been more widely extended, and the possession of them brought within more general reach of the public by the reduction of price, which always follows production on an increased scale.

"The manufacture of pianos has increased remarkably in England, and more particularly in London; but it is even more astonishing to observe the extension of this branch of industry in smaller places, such as Stuttgart, the principal city of Würtemberg. In 1806, Schiedmayer, from Nuremberg, was the sole pianoforte manufacturer in the Suabian capital; there are now no less than thirty-eight thriving houses in this trade who export their instruments, grand, square, and cottage, to many different parts of the world (a large number coming annually to London). But to look again at home, we cannot but be impressed with wonder at the extraordinary production of the house of Messrs. John Broadwood and Sons, who, from 1780 to 1826, made no less than 48,348 pianos, and from the latter year to 1861, the immense number of 75,500, a yet more surprising aggregate. It is reckoned that London alone produces some 23,000 a year; we may therefore assume, without fear of exaggeration, that England, France, Belgium, and Germany, with Austria and Switzerland, do not supply less annually than 60,000 pianos." Since Herr Pauer wrote this, ten years ago, the number of pianofortes manufactured annually in England has greatly increased, and the gross amount may now be stated at little short of 30,000.

Free-reed Instruments.

At the head of this list I must place the Harmonium. Although commonly regarded in England as a new instrument, it has, under some varieties of form and name—such as Harmonica, Physharmonica, Ecline,

Euphonion, Melodion, Seraphine, and the like, been known and used for many years in Germany, France, and England. Either as a disjunct portion, or a component register of the organ itself, it may indeed claim a much remoter origin. Many of the older French organs contain stops of free-reeds identical in principle with those of the harmonium; while in the ancient *regal* we have undoubtedly the prototype of the modern instrument, although the former, probably, differed as widely from the latter, in accuracy of workmanship and purity of tone, as did the rude organ, described by the monk Theophilus in the eleventh century, from the magnificently finished instruments of the present day.

For the description of a free-reed I must borrow the words of Professor Pole: "In the ordinary reed pipe of an organ the sound is produced by the vibration of a thin tongue of metal allowed to beat upon the flattened side of a tube, and so alternately to cover and uncover a slit or opening, through which the air passes into the pipe above. Now, let us suppose that the brass tongue (which in the above case must of course be large enough to cover the opening entirely, and to bear on its margin) be made a little smaller, so as not to cover the opening, but just to enter into it without touching. The consequence will be that when the reed is set in vibration, it will no longer *beat* against the plate, as in the ordinary organ reed, but will oscillate *freely*, entering the opening and leaving it again at each vibration. It is obvious that, since the tongue is made to close the opening as nearly as possible, it will check, in every vibration, the current of air passing through, in the same manner as the beating-reed; and the effect will therefore be, as in that case, a series of pulsations in the air, producing a musical tone." This disposition of reed is called a Free-reed, and it has several advantages over the beating one, which have led to its adoption in the class of instruments which I am describing.

The modern revival of the free-reed dates early in the present century, and is due to the efforts of a M. Grénié who, about 1810, constructed two instruments on this principle, one of which was sent to the Conservatoire, the other to the Convent of the Sacré-Cœur, at Paris. In 1827, three stops on the free-reed principle were introduced into the organ at Beauvais Cathedral, by a workman of M. Grénié's named Cosyn, and who was again employed in 1829 by M. Sebastian Erard, to execute a stop of a similar kind in an organ built by him for the Tuileries. The credit of constructing the first instrument of this kind, i. e. an organ having a free-reed stop without pipes, is due to England. This instrument was made by Mr. Green, of Soho Square, and called the Seraphine; it had a compass of five octaves, and from its cheapness and small size soon became popular. It was extensively manufactured and considerably improved in France, and under different names has culminated in perfection under that of the Harmonium.

The mechanical parts of the harmonium are very simple. The keys open valves by which the wind from the bellows is allowed to act on the reeds, and the draw-stops open or close the communications with a whole row of reeds together. The air is supplied to the reeds from the reservoir bellows; but as this wind (as in the organ) is produced by constant pressure, the tones are of uniform or equal strength. By the use of the expression stop, the wind communication to the reeds is cut off from the reservoir bellows and opened to the feeders. Thus, it will be understood, by using different degrees of force in the pressure of the feet (the bellows of the harmonium being blown by the performer) the effects of soft and loud may be obtained at pleasure. Thus the harmonium possesses an entirely new property, which is not found in the organ. To use the words of Professor Pole: "The beating-reed gives but the one grade of tone it is voiced to, without variation, and will only speak properly under the pressure of wind it is originally constructed for; but the free-reed has the valuable peculiarity that by varying the pressure of the wind, the power of the tone may be varied at pleasure, without altering the pitch. The reason of this is found in the well-known fact that the vibrations of an elastic body will be isochronous, no matter what the extent of the oscillation may be. The effect of a more powerful wind is to increase the arc of vibration, and the greater impetus of the passing air gives a more powerful tone; but since the vibrations are performed in the same time, the pitch of the note remains uniform. By simple contrivances, therefore, for varying the pressure of the wind, the free-reed may be made to give any gradation of *piano* and *forte*, and to produce any *crescendo* and *diminuendo* effects that may be desired."

In 1842, M. Martin, of Paris, introduced an improvement of considerable importance in this instrument, with a view of remedying a defect previously existing to some extent, i. e. the want of promptness in articulation. This was the stop called *Percussion*. It may properly be termed the *pianoforte* action, as it consists in a series of hammers attached to the keys, similar to those used in the latter instrument, which give a gentle blow to the reeds at the moment of striking the key or opening the valve. The effect of this is to make the note speak with rapidity and precision. It is of indispensable use in instruments intended for the drawing room, and of the greatest possible advantage in performing the higher classes of church music. In fact, this is the most important invention yet applied to the harmonium.

In 1858 several improvements were made by Mr. Evans in the details connected with this instrument, one of which was a peculiar contrivance for setting large reeds in motion at the instant that the key is struck. He also invented a self-acting blowing machine. This consists of a number of small bellows feeders, worked by clockwork, which can be set in motion or stopped at pleasure. But the greatest improvement made by Mr. Evans is in the tone of his instruments, giving them an organ-like quality. This is effected chiefly by using reeds of various thicknesses. In this respect he has been followed lately by the French makers. A few years later (1864) Mr. Gilmour, of Glasgow, invented an improved system of swell, by which the sound can be increased or diminished with extraordinary ease. It seems that "in order to gain complete power of modulation, a box is placed over the reed-chest, fitting closely, so that the sound is as effectively confined as if the instrument were shut into another room; in the top of this box two openings are cut, and valves and lids placed over them; these covers have arms attached to them, which, being made to turn on a bridge and projecting over the action towards the back of the instrument, the full power of the sound may be obtained by pressing down the extreme ends of these arms, and so opening the lids or covers which confine the sound. Part of Mr. Gilmour's patent is for connecting these arms with the wind reservoir, by means of an elastic cord, so that when a moderate supply of wind is used, the covers remain closed; but as it (the reservoir) expands, the elastic cords open the covers, and thus produce a most perfect swell." In the same year, Mr. Dawes, of Leeds, invented his "melody attachment," its effect being to give a perfectly clear and distinct additional melody or, in other words, additional tones to the melody, with power and variety in proportion to the number of melody stops employed, thus producing the effect of one or more solo instruments being used in addition to the full harmony of the accompanying portion of the instrument. This is effected by causing one or more ranges of reeds to sound the melody note only, to obtain which effect one portion of the instrument is coupled to another. The coupler is made upon what is technically called the "pneumatic lever" principle, but considerably modified. An entirely new or different arrangement of the small inlet or leading valves or pallets is used. These are so constructed, that the condensed air employed to actuate the levers is obliged to pass through, or from one valve to the next, in succession downwards, or in the direction from right to left, so that the coupler wind-chest is, as it were, divided into a series of small chambers, one for each pallet. These chambers communicate with each other in such manner, that the sliding or opening of any one or more of the pallets shall close the openings in the division next below itself; thus the communication from one chamber to the other through the entire series is continuous only so long as the keys are unpressed, so that in playing upon the instrument, the continuity of this wind-chest or series of chambers and the compressed air therein ceases at, or immediately below, the upper top or melody note of the music.

The modern harmonium owes much of its excellence to the untiring exertions of Mr. Kemp, of the firm of Chappell and Co., whose numerous improvements in the mechanical details, sizes of reeds, &c., have been carried out by the house of Alexandre and Co., of Paris. To him we are indebted for the *Alexandre organ*, an instrument lately introduced to the public, in which the reedy tone of the former instrument is replaced by one of a soft and diapason-like quality more resembling that produced from pipes.

The latest invention in the class of free-reed instruments is the *American organ*. It differs from the harmonium in the manner in which the sound is produced. In the latter, as we have seen, pressure of wind is used to set the reed in vibration. The American organ, on the contrary, has a double exhaust bellows, and the air is sucked through the reeds. In other words, the harmonium reeds are set in motion by the air *within* the instrument. In the American organ they are set in motion by the air *outside* rushing in to fill up a vacuum caused by the action of the bellows. By this latter process a rounder and less reedy tone is produced, but the instrument bears no comparison in variety of tone and expression to that from which it is derived. Another peculiarity of the new invention is the *automatic swell*. This swell takes the place of the ordinary expression stop. In this arrangement, as we have before explained, the wind is cut off from the bellows and remains directly under the command of the feet placed on the two footboards; according to the pressure of the feet, heavy or light, so is the tone loud or soft. With the automatic swell, the player by the blowing alone, can obtain any degree of tone from the loudest to the softest; this is regulated by the quickness of motion of the blowing pedals, and no break can possibly occur. The *tremolo* of the harmonium is replaced in the American organ by the *Vox Humana*. The former is produced by the wind passing through a very small loaded bellows fixed on the top of the sound-board, before it can reach the vibrators; when this little bellows is distended, some wind escapes, and the top of it being loaded immediately falls, alternately rising and falling from the wind supplied by the large bellows beneath; the wind thus going to the reeds in puffs produces the tremolo. The new tremolo is obtained by the motion of a rapidly revolving fan acted upon by the bellows, and setting in motion the external air or waves of sound after they have left the reeds. The action of this is very clever and perfect, and the effect produced is decidedly good.

The American organ is prospering in this country, and makers are rapidly springing up to supply the demand. The London-made instruments are in no way inferior to the celebrated "Mason and Hamlin" organs.

The harmonium was introduced into this country in 1846, and its sale has steadily increased year by year. The demand for instruments of this class (including the American organ and the Alexandre organ) at the present time is computed at 15,000 annually, a large proportion being of the smaller kind, i.e. those selling at from four to twenty guineas. A number of these instruments are made in London, a few in Germany and America, but by far the greater portion are manufactured in France.

Another result of the use of the free-reed, is the invention of the English concertina. This popular instrument was first patented in 1829 by Messrs. Wheatstone. It was the invention of Professor Wheatstone, by whose scientific labours many valuable improvements in the construction of instruments with vibrating tongues, or plates, have been effected. The principle of the production of the tone from the action of wind upon metallic tongues is the same as in the harmonium. The English concertina is capable of producing the most complex harmonies, and the most difficult violin or flute music can be performed on it. Its compass is three octaves and a half, and it possesses not only a complete chromatic scale, but also an *enharmonic* scale; it having two separate tones, for instance, for the notes G sharp and A flat, and D sharp and E flat. From this fact, as well as through the flexibility of the bellows, the chords are in better tune than is generally the case with instruments of fixed sounds. When first invented, the tongues of the concertina were made of a composite metal; but steel tongues are now used as producing a purer tone and being more durable.

Another instrument has sprung out of this—the Anglo-German concertina. It is very inferior in every respect to the original, but is nevertheless very extensively used and has taken the place of the accordion. Each key produces two chords, one by drawing the bellows outward, another by pressing them inward; so that each instrument has twice as many notes as there are keys. It is very easy to play, and on that account is perhaps the most popular instrument under manufacture. It is of great commercial importance to Saxony and Vienna, where 400,000 are manufactured annually. In England there are only two great makers, Messrs. Lachenal and Chidley (late Wheatstone), and the manufacture is about 5000 annually.

Wind Instruments of Wood.

Wind instruments of all classes have been greatly improved in the present century, but perhaps the one that stands pre-eminent in this respect is the flute. To explain its present position, it will be sufficient to go back only to the commencement of the last century, when the flute was almost excluded from orchestras on account of its manifold imperfections. At this time it was an instrument without keys, played straight to the mouth and called " flute à bec." The German flute was of the same construction, but with the mouth on the side, and hence named " flauto traverso." This instrument had but six holes, which were stopped by the first three fingers of each hand. From these holes, combined with the note given by the entire tube—that is when all the notes were closed—was produced the diatonic scale of D major. The first change was made by Philibert, a Frenchmen, who added a key called the D key. This constituted the one-keyed flute, or flute with seven holes, as seen in the one-keyed flute of the present day. Joseph Tacet, an Englishman, added three keys, constituting the four-keyed flute, in order to give the chromatic scale with more correctness. To Quantz (1720–1770) is ascribed the method of lengthening and shortening the head-joint, so as to raise or lower the pitch of the instrument. The two long keys were subsequently added to extend the compass, the tube being thus lengthened. The long F key and B shake key were then added, making the flute an eight-keyed instrument, which it at present remains.

Additional keys have been tried, but they only increased the complication without adding to the capabilities of the instrument.

The next thing to consider was the improvement of the tone and intonation, and this required a somewhat different construction. Captain Gordon's name is associated with these attempts, as well as that of M. Boehm, of Munich. To estimate rightly the value of the new invention it will be necessary to describe the old system of construction, and this I shall do in the words of the Rev. W. Cazalet, an associate juror in the Exhibition of 1851. "In the old system, the head was a cylinder and the body a cone, by which contrivance the sound made at the embouchure was lost in the cylinder, and stopped in its passage along the tube. From the conical shape it was impossible to fix the proper points for the holes, as the vibrations were necessarily rendered uncertain, for the shape of the cone itself is one entirely of experiment, and the difficulty was increased as the thickness of the wood at the holes enters into the tube length. The keys also were made to shut, which tended to throw the holes more and more out of their places, for where a key is left closed below a hole, the sound is necessarily flattened, and the hole then must be placed nearer the embouchure to remedy the defect. Under such a complication of misconstruction, it is no wonder that the flute should have been an instrument almost under ban, and except in the hands of some player whose skill enabled him to counteract some of these imperfections, it was a very unsatisfactory instrument." The result of the new experiments (about 1847) was, that the construction of the flute was reversed. The body is now a cylinder and the head a cone. The object of this is obvious. The sound made at the embouchure is collected into a focus in the head, which in this shape becomes a reflector, and projected in full and equal proportions along the tube, which in the cylinder form becomes in character like a monochord, in which the divisions of tone can be accurately made. The distance of the tones for the chromatic scale is about an inch and a half, making a small allowance for the length as the holes approach the embouchure. Another material change was, that the keys were all made open keys, so that the tube was open below each hole in fingering. The principle of construction was now established, and perfect equality of tone and correct intonation for the first time gained upon this instrument. This system is not only applicable for flutes, but has been modified to apply to other instruments, such as the oboe, clarionet, &c.

In carrying out this extensive alteration, M. Boehm cramped the action of the left hand upon the keys. But this imperfection has been remedied by Mr. Carte, who introduced an improved mechanism which set free the thumb and little finger of the left hand, and thus not only is all difficulty avoided, but the powers of execution greatly extended. Mr. Carte's flutes are largely manufactured, and they are justly considered to be very superior instruments.

The "Siccama" flute (so named from its inventor), is an instrument of considerable excellence. The improvements (which exist chiefly in the facilities of fingering) are of too technical a nature to describe in these pages. It is sufficient to say, that by the combination of fingerings some of the difficult scales, such as F sharp major, C sharp major, and in short all those of extreme difficulty in the ordinary flute, are rendered almost as easy to play as the scale of D major; whilst chord and arpeggio passages (almost impossible to execute with extreme neatness on the ordinary flute) are rendered on the "Siccama" flute perfectly facile. It may be added, that on this instrument the size and position of the holes, and the mathematical proportions of the bore, are the result of minute calculation.

The "Equisonant" flute, invented by the late Mr. Clinton, is much esteemed, and deservedly so. It will be remembered, as I have already shown, that two kinds of bore have been used for the interior of the instrument. The bore adopted by Mr. Clinton differs from both these, for reasons now to be explained.

Taking the human voice for a model, it will be found that every different sound has a different size or diameter of the larynx. Musical instruments are based upon the same principle; for instance, the pipes of an organ are gradually shortened in the ascending scale, though it should be distinctly borne in mind that the mere act of shortening is not sufficient, for they must also *vary in diameter*. A similar change of diameter is observable on the strings of a pianoforte, harp, &c.; in short, it is the unerring principle of nature. If a flute be made with a cylindrical bore, it follows that every sound must have the same diameter of tube, and consequently be in direct opposition to nature. The equisonant flute is bored upon the principle of nature, each note having its true and natural diameter of tube, hence the notes are equal throughout; in addition to which, the recent alterations in the mechanism admit of the holes remaining open for the fundamental notes, namely, from the lowest C natural to C sharp in the third space; also the notes in the second octave, by which an increased volume of tone is obtained. The holes are made as large as possible, but without injury to the third octave. In the construction of open-keyed flutes hitherto, the object has been to make the holes extremely large, in order to render the tone of the fundamental notes as loud as possible, or in other words, to concentrate all the force into the two first octaves. Now, although that plan is to a certain extent fascinating upon the first trial of an instrument, it is eventually found to render the upper notes too sharp, thin in quality, and uneven. In the next place, the fingering necessary for the open-keyed system renders many passages difficult and rugged, and others almost insurmountable. These faults are obviated on the equisonant, for, although it is in effect an open-keyed flute, for the tone of the first and second octaves, it remains as before a shut-keyed flute for the system of fingering, and for the notes in the third octave; the mechanism of the right-hand part being unconnected with the left, each of the upper notes have their natural vent holes or nodes, rendering them full, clear, and perfectly in tune in every key, an advantage of the utmost importance, and quite unattainable upon any other system.

The number of flutes annually manufactured, taking the instrument in all its varied forms, perhaps, does not exceed 1000; and out of this number a large proportion are the ordinary instruments of eight keys, used in the army, and for general purposes. As a solo instrument, the flute may be said to have seen its best days.

The researches of M. Boehm into the acoustical properties of tubes, and his adjustment of the finger-holes of wind instruments into correct numbers and measurements, have been of essential advantage in the construction of the clarionet, oboe, and bassoon. The holes being now correct in size and position, these instruments have acquired a perfection in tone and tuning never before attained. The key mechanism, as in the flute, has also been improved in all these instruments, giving facility and precision to the execution, and by which the former difficulty of reaching and stopping the holes at great distances, or of large sizes, is now entirely surmounted.

The clarionet was invented towards the end of the seventeenth century. At first it had but one key, and was very rarely used on account of its numerous imperfections, though the beauty of its tones induced artists to attempt improvements in its construction. The number of keys was gradually increased to five, but when arrived at this point it still offered but few resources. It nevertheless remained in this state from 1770 to 1787, when a sixth key was added. The number of its keys was finally increased to fourteen, but all the defects of the instrument still remained, until a better system of acoustics was brought to bear upon its construction. The mechanism for releasing the thumb and little finger, invented by Mr. Carte (and briefly described in my notice of the flute), may be particularly noticed as being applied to the clarionet, oboe, and bassoon, with great advantage. Recently a most important improvement, patented by Mr. S. A. Chappell, has been effected in the clarionet. It consists of a new open C sharp key, which entirely removes the difficulty, known to all clarionet players, inseparable from the long B natural and C sharp keys, and renders the performance of music bearing a signature of one or more sharps, or more than three flats, as easy of execution as if written in the key of C natural. It also admits of an easy performance of many passages and shakes that are quite impracticable on the Boehm clarionet. These instruments are largely manufactured by Mr. Chappell for the army. Tenor and bass clarionets are now used in military bands, sometimes as extra instruments, or the former for the fourth clarionet part, and the latter as a substitute for the bassoon.

The oboe remained for a long time in a state of imperfection, which prevented it from being employed in the orchestra, except for the music of rural festivals. Keys were first added to it about the end of the seventeenth century, and a French maker, about 1780, further improved it in this respect. The instrument as now manufactured has from twelve to seventeen keys, which, with the improved tube and mathematically correct holes, render it as perfect as need be desired.

The bassoon, which belongs to the same family as the oboe, it being the bass of that instrument, has undergone many modifications since its invention in the first half of the sixteenth century. It has gained perhaps more than any other instrument from being constructed according to M. Boehm's system. The merit of applying the latter has been claimed by M. Sax, of Paris, but it is certainly due to Mr. Cornelius Ward, who patented it in 1853.

Wind Instruments of Brass.

The Exhibition of 1851 contained an unusual number of brass instruments, England, France, and the German States contributing almost exclusively, whilst America, Hamburgh, Canada, Denmark, and even Russia, swelling the list of instruments with fixed tones, such as pianofortes and organs, or instruments of wood, such as flutes and clarionets, &c., do not appear as manufacturers of brass instruments.

The instruments that come under the denomination of "brass" include the horn, cornet-a-pistons, trumpet, ophicleide, trombone, and the whole family of sax-horns.

The horn, invented in France, was originally only used in hunting. The Germans improved it, but it was not employed in the orchestra until the eighteenth century. The sounds, when they could be drawn from it, were five in number, but in 1760, a German named Hampl discovered, that it could be made to produce an additional number by closing with the hand a part of the open portion of the instrument called the pavilion. The discovery was completed a few years later by the addition of a grooved sliding tube, by means of which the precision of the tones could be preserved, when they became too sharp through the warmth of the instrument. It is in the nature of the horn to give only certain sounds in a pure, free, and open tone; the others, which are obtained by the aid of the hand, are much more dull, and are termed *stopped* sounds. Struck with the inconvenience of the common horn, a German named Stœlzel conceived the idea of adding pistons to it, by means of which he opened a communication at will between the column of air in the horn and that of the additional tubes, and thereby obtained open sounds in all the notes. This improvement, which has been brought to perfection by modern makers of brass instruments, has been of great advantage, especially in military music. The Kœnig horn with three pistons, invented by the late Hermann Kœnig, possesses a tone very similar to that of the French horn, for which instrument it is universally admitted to be the best substitute.

The cornet-a-pistons was the result of improvements made in the French horn. It is merely an adaptation of the piston mechanism to the German post-horn, known in military circles as the little cornet. Mr. Distin, whose instruments are of the highest description of excellence, has invented a separate double valve, for the purpose of letting the water out of the instrument. The cornet-a-pistons, being a favourite instrument with amateurs, is largely manufactured both in France and England.

The trumpet is the soprano of the horn, sounding an octave higher than that instrument. Its sounds are modified for the changes of key in the same way as those of the horn—that is, by means of additional tubes. Many attempts have been made, within the last forty years, to increase the resources of the trumpet, but without any corresponding success. At length an Englishman conceived the idea of adding keys to it, like those of the clarionet or oboe, and his experiments for that purpose were crowned with success; but it was found that he had created a new instrument, which in the quality of its tone had little resemblance to the trumpet. The principle of the construction of keyed trumpets being once discovered, it was soon perceived that it might be applied to other instruments of the same kind, but of greater dimensions, which should be the alto, tenor, and bass of the trumpet. This new family of brass instruments has received the name of ophicleides.

The trombone is capable of giving all the notes of the scale in open sounds, by means of a slide, which is moved by the performer in order to lengthen or shorten the sonorous tube. Recently, pistons or valves, have been added to it, and the bell has been somewhat enlarged. The former addition renders it easier to play, but at a sacrifice of tone. The trombone, however, with these alterations, is manufactured for the army, where the objection which I have mentioned is of little importance.

The modern makers of wind instruments have turned their attention to the improvement of the wind course, as the "regulating medium," particularly in valved instruments. M. Perrinet, of Paris, seems to deserve the credit of having, about thirty-five years since, first materially improved the construction of valved instruments; and the English have been very successful in carrying these improvements still further; thus the equitrilateral valves, invented by Mr. Oates, of Lichfield, show the improvement which he effected in the wind-course of brass instruments, avoiding many of the numerous angles by the action of the piston.

M. Sax, of Paris, has done more for brass wind instruments than any manufacturer of the present century. These improvements and inventions are obtained from their remodelled proportions, proving that it is not the quality of the metal brought into vibration by the air-blast which influences to any great extent the quality of the tone produced. The so-called "sax-horns" and "sax-trumpets" possess a quality and richness of tone unheard before their introduction. Their invention has caused a total revolution in military music. Both in the theatre and the concert room, the two extremities of this vast instrumental scale can be introduced with great advantage. The sax-horns (double bass, E flat, and B flat) have left ophicleides very far in arrear, and the small treble sax-horn in B flat is the only brass instrument known, that can reach with certainty and just intonation the notes of the upper octave of the flute.

M. Gautrot, of Paris, is the inventor of the system known as the "equitonic system," by which a true intonation in the lower tones of brass instruments is obtained. This invention is one of the greatest improvements which has been made in modern days in connection with this subject, inasmuch as a perfect intonation in the lowest register has, until M. Gautrot invented his system, been found impossible. To indicate this invention in a few words, take as an illustration a bass sax-horn in B flat and F. This instrument is furnished with three pistons in the usual position, and two others at the side, worked with the left hand, which I will number 1 to 5, and with three columns of air. The fourth piston being pressed down opens the second column of air in connection with the first three pistons, and lowers the notes one-fourth. The fifth piston opens the third column of air, lowers the instrument by a major third, and the other notes produced by three first pistons by a minor sixth. The three first pistons are always tuned according to the ordinary system, so that the player, unused to the equitonic system, can treat the instrument in the ordinary way, until he has mastered such difference of fingering as the new system demands. This improvement in brass instruments of low register, has been adopted by Mr. Distin with considerable success.

The demand for brass instruments has of late years been considerably on the increase, which may be attributed to the ease with which command is now obtained over them by the use of valves, the less force required for the air-blast, consequent on the better form of the instrument, and their present comparative cheapness.

CUTLERY.

By F. Callis (Sheffield).

The art of making cutting instruments is undoubtedly one of great antiquity. Man, in his most primitive state, felt his need of them; and they are amongst the earliest weapons which he is recorded to have used. But although the art is so closely associated with his personal comfort and convenience, and with his various pursuits in life, it was for ages very much neglected and allowed to remain comparatively undeveloped. The knife and the razor were in use amongst the Hebrews before the time of Abraham; and they were not unknown to the Egyptians. Like those subsequently used by the Romans, the blades were of bronze, and the handles of wood or stone. The only cutting instruments known apparently to the ancient Britons were the shell or stone celts. During the middle ages, considerable progress was made by some of the chief cities of the Continent in the manufacture of the sword and other similar warlike weapons, and attention was also given to the more peaceful art of making cutlery. When Englishmen began to manufacture for themselves is uncertain, but when Elizabeth came to the throne, the trade was established in London, Sheffield, and other parts of the country; and with the view of encouraging it, restrictions were placed upon the importation of such goods. The London cutlers had then been incorporated by Royal Charter for more than one hundred years, and were enjoying a large proportion of the trade. The superiority of the goods made at Sheffield had, however, already asserted itself, and had attracted attention. Chaucer had immortalized the "Shefeld thwytel"; and Gilbert, Earl of Shrewsbury, had so high an appreciation of them, that he sent to his friend Lord Burghley "a case of Hallomshire whittells, beinge suche fruictes as his pore country afforded with fame throughout the realm."

The cutlers at Sheffield at that time were little better than serfs. The trade was hampered by regulations of the most repressive character, and the most scanty remuneration was given for the work performed. No one at that period would have ventured to predict that this small wretched village with its indigent population, would one day be the chief seat of the cutlery trade; and that its goods would become famous throughout the world. The reasons why it has become so are obvious. Apart from the general excellence of the goods made there, the town possessed great natural advantages, which were more highly appreciated before the days of railways and steam power than now. There was an abundance of water power, and coal was within easy reach, while iron, and subsequently steel, were easily obtainable. The inhabitants availing themselves of these favourable conditions, laid themselves out to develop the trade and to meet the increasing wants of the age. They secured and maintained the lead, and even now the town remains without a rival in the production of the higher classes of goods. The frequent and protracted strikes which have taken place amongst the workmen, the limitation of apprentices, and other kindred causes, have of late years seriously interfered with the progress of the trade, and in many instances have driven it into the hands of French and German rivals.

It is generally conceded that the earliest specimen of English cutlery, of which we have any definite knowledge, is the "whittle"; and an exceedingly rude and inconvenient weapon was it as compared with those of the present day; the blade being of bar steel, and fastened in a handle of wood or cow's horn. It continued in use down to the seventeenth century. The "jack knife" followed, and was a slight improvement upon the whittle, inasmuch as the blade was made to shut into a groove in the handle, and when open was supported by a "tang," not unlike the tang of a razor. There was little variety of pattern, and the workmanship was rough and unskilful; and amongst the poor ill-paid cutlers, there appeared to be no spirit of invention. The trade was at a stand, and needed introducing into it men with higher taste and more cultivated genius to give it stimulus; and through the representations of the Duke of Alva, those advantages were secured to it. Many of the Protestants who fled from the Netherlands, came to this country and met with a cordial reception from Elizabeth and her Court. Such as were cutlers were sent down by the Earl of Shrewsbury to Sheffield, where they introduced their inventions. With them the art of making cutlery had not advanced so far as to have led to the discovery of the "spring," but they made their blades to close with a catch pin working in a segment of a circle. They used other material than wood and horn for handles, and improved the ornamentation of them; they increased the number of blades in a knife, and made them more convenient for general use; but the invention, which above all others was to give the greatest impetus to the trade, had not yet been made. It may be mentioned incidentally, that some of the refugees from the Netherlands settled in Sheffield and the neighbourhood, and their descendants dwell there to this day.

By whom, when, and where the spring knife was first made, is not certain. Amongst a very interesting collection of old cutlery in the possession of a gentleman at Sheffield is a large single blade spring knife, with the handle of brass-mounted oak, and upon the roughly ground steel blade is a trade mark. It was probably a butler's or sportsman's knife, as at the bottom of the handle and closing into it there is a short corkscrew. No improvement is shown either in the pattern or the workmanship; its chief characteristic being, that it shuts with a spring. It is believed to have been made in Sheffield, about the year 1600, and several eminent antiquaries have pronounced it the oldest known specimen of a spring knife. Notwithstanding the impetus which the trade received from the introduction of the inventions of the refugees from the Netherlands, and the still more important discovery of the spring, it was almost inconceivably slow in developing. During the seventeenth century, nearly the whole of the cutlery that was made for the use of the English people was of the plainest possible description. A little ornamentation of the goods manufactured for the Spanish market and the islands of the Mediterranean was attempted. The scales were dyed, and flowers and other devices were carved upon them. The eminent firm of Joseph Rodgers and Sons, of Sheffield, which has been established nearly two centuries, has in its possession a set of samples made in 1735. They are, as compared with the goods now produced, exceedingly plain and sadly wanting in design, although really good in quality. At this period, buffalo and other horns came into general use, and ivory and pearl were used for more expensive goods.

The trade may be said to have entered upon its new era about 1820, when the celebrated "Wharncliffe knife" was invented. As the story goes, the first Lord Wharncliffe and his relative Archdeacon Corbett were sipping their wine one day after dinner, when the conversation turned upon cutlery, and the little invention shown in the manufacture of spring knives. Not wishing to criticise where they could not improve, they laid their heads together, and with the assistance of a practical man succeeded in producing a new pattern knife. It was handed to the Messrs. Rodgers, who adopted it, and introduced to the world the "Wharncliffe knife," upon the basis of which the greater part of the spring-knife cutlery, intended for the home market, is now made. Still more singular are the circumstances attending the invention of the "fly knife." It is stated that, many years ago, a gentleman was attacked and robbed by two men near London, and the injuries which he received terminated fatally. Before his death, he said, that had he been able to open his knife with one hand, he could have successfully defended himself against his assailants. That remark came to the knowledge of a cutler at Sheffield, named Milner, who succeeded in inventing a knife the blade of which flew open, when a spring in the handle was pressed; just such a weapon as the murdered man had desired. This form of knife, however, is expensive, and has never come into general use. There are one or two firms in Sheffield, notably Messrs. Rodgers and Messrs. Brookes and Crookes, who have been exceedingly successful in producing these "specialities." Indeed to this class of goods, they have devoted special and unremitting attention. Their motto has been, "concentration and practical utility, combined with the highest art and the most perfect workmanship." Having heard the expressed desire for a good knife that contained in addition to all the ordinary blades, a railway carriage key, a champagne opener, a corkscrew, a turnscrew, a button hook, and so forth, they have been engaged for weeks in producing such a knife. A ramble in the garden amongst the flowers and fruit trees, has resulted in the invention of the "florist" with steel and ivory pruners, budding blades, saw, and magnifying glass. The sportsman, whether hunting, shooting, or fishing, has his knife, containing almost every instrument that he can possibly need in his favourite amusement. For the lovers of the "fragrant weed," there is the "smoker," replete with stopper and fork, picker and striker. Then a perfect gem is the "lady's knife," as it contains almost every article required upon the toilet table. Many of the most novel specimens of this class of goods have originated in suggestions from buyers, who have asked to have made for them, knives containing certain instruments of a particular shape or for a special purpose; and knives of new design have been invented as the result of their request.

The table knife and fork have a history extending back far beyond that of the spring knife. In the days of Athelstane the Anglo-Saxons used them, but they were undoubtedly luxuries and possessed only by the few, and indeed continued to be so down to the early part of the last century. It was no uncommon circumstance for persons attending weddings and dinners, to provide themselves with their own knives and forks, as mine host was not expected to have sufficient for the use of all. Gradually their need was more widely felt, and manufacturers prepared to supply the growing demand. The scope for improvement in table cutlery has been much more limited than in spring goods; but almost all that it was possible to do in the way of variety of pattern, elegance of design, and excellence of workmanship, has been accomplished.

The scissor branch of the trade has afforded a much wider field for improvement, and it has developed accordingly. Like other articles of cutlery, its early history is left very much in doubt. A few specimens are found amongst collections of old cutlery, somewhat rude in design and rough in execution, though they embody the principle which has since been so successfully worked out. They are now manufactured in endless variety of pattern, of all sizes, from one-sixteenth of an inch to twenty-four inches in length, for very different uses, and ranging in price from 3d. per dozen pairs to 20l. the single pair. The perfection to which this class of goods can be brought, has been shown in the specimens which have been occasionally manufactured for exhibition. They have had introduced into them the highest style of design and the most elaborate ornamentation; practical utility being combined with both.

The great antiquity of the razor is placed beyond all possible doubt. Probably the earliest reference to it is in the book of Numbers, where Moses is instructed to inform the children of Israel, that upon the head of the man who had taken the vow of a Nazarite, "no razor should come" during the days of his separation. Again in Judges, the Psalms, and other books of the Old Testament, reference is made to the same instrument. Occasionally on Egyptian sculptures a figure may be seen with a razor; and it is also alluded to in Homer. The Greeks and Romans shaved as a mark of civilization, and from their time it has never fallen entirely into disuse. There have been periods, as during the time of the Charles', and even within the last twenty years, when it has not been popular to shave, but the movement which cast the razor aside has passed away, to allow it again to come into more general use. The mere form of the razor, judging by

M

ancient specimens and sketches, has not passed through any material change; but in the details of its manufacture, it has undergone great improvement, as well as in the quality of steel used for the blades and the material for the handles. The carver, the etcher, and the experienced workman have also found full scope for their abilities in the ornamenting and beautifying of the razor. To the man who shaves, there can scarcely be a greater luxury than to possess a razor that will cut well, without causing him the slightest pain or unpleasantness. Considering the care that is required in the manufacture of the razor, and the excellence of the steel of which the blade should be composed, such essentials as those referred to can hardly be expected in a common or cheap razor. Indeed they are not always to be secured in the best goods, as there is scarcely an article of cutlery made which is so uncertain in its quality as a razor. It is the experience of one who has given much attention to the subject, "that due proportion, form, temperature, fitness, and regularity of concavity must all combine to produce an excellent razor." Notwithstanding, the demand for fine razors in this country is comparatively small. The chief markets for these goods are America, India, and Australia. The Chinese, who are great shavers, use a very peculiar form of razor, and refuse to give it up. Efforts have been made by one or two of our leading razor manufacturers to open up closer relations with them; and with a view of doing so, they have sent out goods made after their own pattern, but have not succeeded in their object to any extent. Very curious stories are told as to the way in which the goods of particular houses have obtained reputation. For instance, nearly one hundred years ago, a regiment of soldiers was passing through Sheffield, and a local manufacturer presented to each officer a pair of what were then considered elegant razors. The officers accepted the gifts and promised to recommend the goods, wherever they went. They did so, and the house gained a reputation, which it has had the good fortune to continue to enjoy.

The cutlery trade embraces the manufacture of silver and silver-plated fish, dessert, butter, and other knives and forks, with handles of pearl, ivory, and such costly material. By stamping, chasing, and other processes, the ornamentation of this class of goods has been carried to a state of great perfection, and they command a large sale both in the English and foreign markets. Pencil cases with blades, scissors, rules, and other instruments, and an almost endless variety of similar goods are now produced in the shops of the cutlers.

The endeavours that have been made to introduce art into the cutlery trade have not been attended with as much success as could be desired. About 1730, engraving of the shields and bolsters of pen and pocket knives, and of the blades of table knives and razors, was commenced, but was received with little favour. An opinion even obtained that it was intended to hide some defect in the instrument. Fifty years ago, the art of bluing, gilding, and etching the blades was introduced from the Continent, and for some years was extensively adopted, but it has since gone out of fashion. Deep etching is now used for putting arms, crests and so forth, upon table cutlery; and it would be capable of being applied to an almost unlimited extent, if there were men in the trade to develop it, and if a market could be found for the articles so ornamented. But customers too frequently decline to pay for both utility and ornament, however small the difference in cost may be; and the etchers, as a rule, are so miserably remunerated, that men with the requisite skill and technical knowledge are rather driven from, than attracted to the trade, which remains for the most part in the hands of men with mere mechanical ability. A few years ago, the system of etching by means of transfers from copper plates, as in the pottery trade, was introduced into the cutlery trade, and is now more generally adopted than the old practice of using the etching needle.

In 1849, a more systematic attempt was made to combine art with utility in the manufacture of cutlery, and several of the best London artists were employed, such as John Bell, Daniel Maclise, Reuben, Townrow, and others. They produced some very chaste and beautiful patterns, some of which were adopted by Messrs. Rodgers, and were brought out under the superintendence of the artists. The effort was not appreciated as was hoped, and the experience gained was, that the introduction of art work into articles of general use made them more costly than people wished. The movement was not altogether barren of good results, as it enabled English manufacturers to make a very imposing display of goods at the Exhibition of 1851, and to more than hold their own against the world. The "Norfolk knife," perhaps more than any other, showed the perfection to which the art of cutlery had been brought. It contained a great number of blades, on which were etchings of Her Majesty, and other royal personages, of Windsor Castle and other residences. On one side of the handle, which was of carved pearl, was a boar hunt, and on the converse a stag hunt. The backs of the blades were exquisitely ornamented. Side by side with this knife in Messrs. Rodgers' show room, is another containing no less than 1876 blades and instruments, all perfect, and no two alike. Upon such articles, and the expensive specimens of cutlery generally, the highest art and the most skilled workmanship have been expended; but not to any very appreciable extent upon the ordinary class of goods in every-day use. A person will purchase an ornamented article for a present, but for his own use he buys "something plain and that will cut." The same object has been aimed at by offering premiums to the workmen for inventions or new patterns; but they have failed to produce anything novel in character or new in design. The complaint is made, that it is in a great measure attributable to the action of the men, that the trade has not developed much more rapidly and widely than it has. They are paid by "piece," and demand extra remuneration for everything that can be termed "extra" in a knife, altogether irrespective of the time that it may take to make it. The misfortune appears to be, that the rate of wages is far too low; and they endeavour to recoup themselves for this, by charging all that they possibly can for "extras." A manufacturer may devote much time and thought to the bringing out of a new pattern, simple in its details and easily made. It may have more "extras," but on the whole will not occupy so much time in making, as one that has fewer. The men look only at the "extras," and ask such a price for making it, as compels the manufacturer to abandon the idea of bringing it out, and it is therefore thrown aside. The men lose good work, and the manufacturer is discouraged in his efforts to improve and extend the trade, as he is unable to tempt business by offering new pattern goods on more reasonable terms.

It is perhaps almost unnecessary to say, that the real practical value of any article of cutlery depends almost entirely upon the quality of the steel of which the blades are formed. If the steel be bad, no matter how highly the blades may be ornamented, the article will afford no pleasure in its use. It is therefore of the first importance with the best makers to secure the highest brands of Swedish iron, to have it carefully converted and melted into double refined cast steel, and then tilted and rolled to the various sizes required.

There are very few trades, in which the principle of subdivision of labour has been more fully carried out, than in the manufacture of cutlery. A knife of the most ordinary character has to pass through a great number of hands and a variety of processes, at each stage of which, judgment and care are required to prevent its eventually turning out a "waster." A glance at these various processes may not be uninteresting. Let us take the table knife, in the production of which the forge is first employed. The forger works in a small room, in which are a hearth, two troughs, one to hold water and the other prepared coke, a small anvil, striking tools, dies and so forth. Taking a bar of steel, he plunges it into the fire, and while working his bellows with the left hand, he, with the right, frequently withdraws the bar, to ascertain when it has attained to a proper heat. In this operation he has to exercise the nicest judgment, for if he allowed it to become overheated, the steel would be " burnt," changed into a sulphuret of iron, and so rendered useless for the purpose required. On the other hand, unless raised to the proper heat, the forger is unable to manipulate it into the proper shape. The skilled forger, however, knows with unerring certainty the precise moment at which to withdraw the bar, and bringing it to the anvil, he, with a few swift strokes of his hammer, forms a blade to any given pattern. From this rod, the blade is then welded to a piece of iron of which the "tang," the part that goes into the handle, and the "bolster," the raised part at the end of the handle, are formed. The tang is quickly beat out by a few strokes with the hammer, and the bolster is shaped in a die. When the latter are of German silver or any other material that cannot be welded to the iron, they have to be riveted afterwards to the tang. This ornamentation of the knife is obtained to some extent at the expense of its utility, inasmuch as the part which should be the strongest is made weak by the perforation.

The blade, having been heated a second time, receives a few finishing touches with the hammer, and then the name of the maker is stamped upon it. The blade is next brought to a high degree of hardness by being raised to a red heat and then plunged into cold water, by which it becomes as "hard as steel," but as brittle as glass, and consequently unfit for use. It requires "tempering," and to secure this, it is again heated until the practised eye of the workman sees it acquire a bluish hue, when he instantly returns it to the water to attain the right degree of flexibility. The blade is now ready for the grinder; and the "hull" in which he works is amongst the most curious sights in the trade, with its clatter of machinery, flying of sparks, and heaps of "wheel swarf." Sitting astride his "horse," the grinder takes a blade, fits it in a wooden case to protect his hands from the heat excited by the friction, and then first grinds the bolster smooth and bright, and afterwards gives the blades a rough preliminary touch on the stone. It is next taken to the smithy, where it is made perfectly straight; and then again ground and whitened. It is now ready to undergo the various processes of lapping, glazing, and polishing, which are performed on different wheels or laps, with the aid of emery and other powders. The finished blade is forwarded to the warehouse, where it is examined, and, if up to the mark in workmanship and according to pattern, it is "passed."

Respecting the manufacture of forks, it will not be necessary to say much. To produce the better descriptions, the forger takes a bar of steel, tilted to three-eighths of an inch square, and first forms the tang, shoulder, and shank, at the end of which he leaves an inch of the square steel, afterwards beating it out flat to the length and width for which the prongs are required. It is then heated until it is soft, and placed in the lower half of a die. The upper half is made to descend upon it with considerable force, and in this way the prongs are roughly formed, ready for the careful filing which they subsequently receive. Great quantities of forks are cast, as being cheaper and more expeditious; but of course they have not the durability of their brethren of the forge. The next step is the grinding, which opens up one of the most painful chapters in the history of the cutlery trade. With few exceptions, other descriptions of cutlery are ground upon stones, which either revolve in water, or have a small jet turned upon them, and in this way the particles that fly from the stone, are prevented from escaping into the room. Forks were for years ground exclusively upon dry stones, and in consequence this branch of trade had come to be regarded as more destructive to human life than almost any other. Public attention was directed to the matter by eminent medical authorities and remedies were suggested, but the men were reluctant to adopt them, although their average age had sunk to twenty-nine, on the ground that if the trade was made more healthy, more labour would be imported into it, and wages, already little enough, would be further reduced. Dr. Holland pointed out that in the rooms in which the men worked, the fine particles of stone and metal rose in clouds and pervaded the atmosphere, inducing disease of the lungs and premature death. At some establishments wet grinding has been adopted, and at others an apparatus consisting of a fan, with a flue to take away the dust from each stone, has been fitted up, and by this means the grinder is protected from inhaling the dust, while the atmosphere of the room is kept pure and healthy,— at least as healthy as in other shops. The mortality amongst the dry grinders has of late years decreased, but not to such an extent as could be desired.

The processes through which the blades for pen and pocket knives pass, differ slightly in detail, but in principle they are very much the same as those described. The bars of steel generally used for razor blades, are half an inch in width and of the thickness of the back of the razor. The end of the bar having been heated, the forger brings it to his anvil and, with extraordinary skill, moulds the blade to the required edge, and then obtains the concave surface by working it on the rounded edge of his anvil. The blade is then severed from the bar, leaving a piece at the end sufficient for the tang, if it is to be of the same material. If not, it is cut flush, and the tang is welded to it as in the case of a table knife. In the smithing process, which comes next, the skill of the workman is shown in hammering the metal until it is perfectly compact, but in giving to the blade its proper form, and a sharp edge. A more perfect form is given to the blade, and the rough coating from the heat is removed by working it on a coarse grindstone. The joint hole is drilled, the name or trade-mark is stamped upon it, and it is ready to be hardened and tempered, by being alternately heated and cooled. It quickly passes through the remaining processes of grinding, lapping, and polishing, and it is then ready to be handled and set.

While the forgers, grinders, and buffers have thus been busily engaged upon the blades, the workmen in other departments have been equally active in preparing the various parts necessary to make the article complete. There are the springs, some of which are forged with the same skill and rapidity as were shown in the production of the blade. Others are "flied"— cut with a single blow out of a sheet of solid steel; and for some uses, equally as good as the forged article. The inner "scales" are of iron, brass, and German silver, and they form the small chambers into which the several blades or instruments shut. An almost endless variety of material is used for the outer scales or coverings, from the common wood or bone to ivory or pearl, richly inlaid with gold, silver, and precious stones, and elaborately carved. Pearl is at once the most beautiful and the most expensive material used for hafting, though difficulty is experienced in finding it of sufficient size to use for the larger classes of goods. Next, in beauty and value, and in much more general use, is ivory. It is a somewhat singular fact, that the handles most in favour with the public are those made from the ivory found in the sands of the great desert, where it had lain so long, that it will crack even from the heat of the workman's hand. It is, however, very opaque, and the uninitiated prefer it for its whiteness. The best and most durable ivory comes from the Angola coast. It has a rich creamy or oily look, and while the other ivory is white at the beginning and turns to a dirty yellow with age, this improves in colour, the longer it is used. It is much better than either the Cape or East Indian ivory. Ivory is obtained from the milk teeth of the elephant, which are about 9 inches long and weigh $1\frac{1}{2}$ lb., and from the large tusks, some of which weigh 160 lb. It is almost matter for surprise where all the ivory comes from, inasmuch as in Sheffield alone, in some years, the tusks of over twenty thousand elephants have been used. In several of them musket balls of silver or gold have been found, showing that the beasts had been fired at by royal personages. Stag horns, the largest and finest of which come from Bavaria, and the horns of the elk, the antelope, rhinoceros, walrus, buffalo, and ox, are all cut up for scales. The leg bones of the giraffe and of the ox are also utilized; and an attempt has been made to use the ribs of the larger fish, but without success, as they were found to be too hard and unworkable. The elephants' tusks and some of the other material are cut up into lengths by machinery, but the great bulk of the work is done by hand labour, not only skill but good judgment being required in the operation. In a single horn or tusk will be found more than half-a-dozen varieties, and one man will operate upon them with greater gain than another. After the materials have been cut to proper sizes and lengths, they are carefully sorted, according to their value and the different kinds of work for which they are intended. For the handles of common goods the horns of cattle are used, and the processes through which they pass in preparation are exceedingly simple. The horns are slit up and laid in little baths of hot water, and when sufficiently soft, they are pressed in a mould to the exact form required, and after being trimmed with a knife, are ready for use. The prices of nearly all these materials have doubled during the past few years, and scales of wood and composition, pressed to imitate stag and buffalo, have been introduced for common goods. In addition to the blades and scales, the list of materials needed by the cutler in putting the knife together, is completed by bolsters, rivets, &c.

There are scarcely half a dozen establishments within whose own walls, all the material requisite for an ordinary knife is worked up from the rough and kept in stock. Herein lies a very great hardship. The man who works for such a house, receives, with an order to make up a certain number of knives, all the material which he requires to complete it. His fellow, who works for a house that does not "stock," has to collect the material from half a dozen warehouses, and thereby loses perhaps half a day before he can begin work. For this extra labour there is no extra remuneration. The giving out of the work to the men is entrusted to the manager, who has to carefully protect the interests of his employers on the one hand, and to do what is right and just to the men on the other; and occupying this unenviable position, he is generally the most abused man about the place. He is usually invested with absolute authority, and is the only medium of communication between the heads of the firm and the men. Without in the slightest degree affecting the interests of his employers, he can by the mode in which he gives out the work, make a difference of several shillings per week in the earnings of a workman. It is therefore to the interests of the men to keep on good terms with him. Either by him, or under his superintendence, the materials required for any particular class of knives are collected and "given out" to the cutler, who takes them to his shop, where in addition to a number of small tools there are "buffs" and "glazers" for polishing portions of the knife. Having "clipped" the several articles to their required lengths, he proceeds to fit them together; a process that requires the greatest possible care and the most experienced manipulation. Next to the excellence or otherwise of the material, the difference between a good knife and a bad one consists in the close-fitting, easy-working of the several parts. So great is the distinction between working upon the best, or upon common goods, that the man who has been accustomed to the one, is unable to gain a livelihood upon the other. When the several parts have been made to fit perfectly together, they have then to be bored, each one separately. This is usually done from the breast with a drill, though greater accuracy is secured by using a small boring machine. The parts are fitted together again and riveted with a hammer on an anvil. At the next step the handle is shaved and then polished on the "buffs," and the springs are brought to a similar state by being put on the "glazers." The handle is now completed, and to protect it from dirt, or from being scratched, it is wrapped in paper with the blades extended. In this state it is returned to the grinder, who glazes, laps, and polishes the blades. It is now ready to receive its final whetting and sharpening on a peculiar kind of stone, the surface of which is oiled. The knife is now finished, and it is returned to the warehouse to be inspected and cleaned, and if approved —perfect in pattern and workmanship—to be passed and wrapped up, having, in the case of an ordinary three-bladed pocket knife, gone through more than one hundred processes.

Much less elaborate is the work of hafting table cutlery. The plan of fastening the tang in the handle by means of resin is perhaps the least satisfactory of all. To rivet the scales on to the full-sized tang is much more secure, but it is only applied to common cutlery. A better system is to carry the tang through the handle and rivet it at the bottom, as it cannot well get loose, and the unsightly part is hidden from view. Messrs. Rodgers have invented and registered a process, whereby the blade is made perfectly secure in the handle. A small spring is fastened to the tang, and as the latter is passed down the hole in the handle, the spring drops into a little nick made in the side, and the blade is thereby secured. A great deal of work is put into razors in the after processes by the carving of the handles, the fluting of the backs of the blades, and other ornamentation. Cases to contain them, carved out of solid ivory and similar costly material, have also been introduced as novelties in the trade.

The earlier processes in the manufacture of steel scissors are exceedingly simple. The forger first heats the end of a bar of flat steel, and with a few strokes of his hammer, forms it into a scissor blade. He then severs the blade from the bar, taking care to leave at the end of it, sufficient steel for the shank and bow. Through the latter he punches a hole sufficiently large to receive the point of his small anvil, and in this manner he works out his bow, rounds the inside, and otherwise perfects it. The shank and bow are then again heated, to be shaped and further improved by filing. The next step is the squaring of the joint and the boring of the hole for the rivet. The blade is now ready to be ground, and when it has undergone that operation, it only remains to be smooth-filed and burnished. When in this state the blades are paired and screwed to form the complete scissors. If they work smoothly together, they are tied round with wire, the screw taken out, and they are hardened and tempered. They are again fastened together, and having undergone various processes such as grinding, glazing, polishing, whetting, and burnishing, they are sent into the warehouse complete. In this, as in the other branches, the men, by long practice, are able to perform their work with wonderful ease and dexterity, whatever the size or shape of the article under manipulation.

The advantages of machinery have been applied to the cutlery trade only to a limited extent. There can be no doubt that the situation of the town of Sheffield, in the very midst of brooks and streams, was one leading cause of its becoming the capital of this important branch of trade, and manufacturers, it will be readily supposed, were not slow to avail themselves of the water power so abundantly provided to their hands. On the banks of these streams, in the midst of the most charming scenery, they erected their grinding wheels, many of which are to this day worked by as strong and healthy a race of men as could be found. Very different indeed was the position of the poor cutlers. They worked at what were called "glazing frames," which were turned with the foot, an old grindstone serving the purpose of a drum. The process was very laborious, and was in fact little better than the treadmill. About 1850 the aid of steam was called in to turn the various wheels and buffs, and much manual labour was thereby saved. Steam has also been applied to the grinding wheels in the town. Some few years ago an attempt was made by Mr. James Drabble to introduce the American system of producing cutlery by machinery, but his efforts were not attended with much success. Messrs. Nixon and Winterbottom, of the Pyramid Works, seeing that there was something in the system, took it up, and have steadily developed it until it has attained to a degree of wonderful perfection. Apart from the marvellous rapidity with which scales and blades and the like can be produced, the system is—and this is its chief and distinguishing characteristic—thoroughly interchangeable. The ordinary practice is, as already explained, to forge each table blade separately, to bore the holes in each tang, and to bore and fit the scales to that tang also separately. Every knife has to have its several parts specially prepared and fitted and kept distinct from all others. Messrs. Nixon and Winterbottom have perfected machinery for accomplishing this work with so much accuracy that, taking a given class of knives or forks, any scale will fit any tang, alike as regards size, pattern, and the perforation of the holes for the rivets. The process is simplicity itself. In the first place, the blades or forks are "flyed," i. e. cut with the die from the solid bar of steel. They are then taken to the punching machine, where two or more holes are made in the tangs. With the left hand the operator puts the tang into the machine, a movement of the foot causes the punches to pierce through it, and with his right hand he removes it. When set to any particular pattern, every tang is perforated exactly like the other, and the same principle is carried out in the perforation of the scales. Interchangeability is thereby secured, and no time whatever is lost in the fitting of part to part. There are other machines for cutting and shaping the scales, the knives of which revolve with amazing rapidity. By another process, the bolsters and caps are run on when the metal is in a liquid state. The whole of these processes are so simple, that they can with ease be carried on by girls and youths. Up to the present time the firm have not extended the system beyond the manufacture of table cutlery, including carvers, desserts, and butcher's knives, and only those of middle qualities. Their experience is, that there is nothing whatever to prevent the application of it to the production of the very best and most expensive of goods. The principle is there; it has only to be applied to the better descriptions of material. For this machine-made cutlery there is a steadily increasing demand; and new markets for it are being continually opened up. Another American practice has also been adopted to a limited extent, of forging table-blades with the aid of the tilt hammer. The process is intermediate between hand-forging and flying, both as regards the quality of the work produced and the time occupied in executing it.

" In the trade generally, there appears to be no particular antipathy to or prejudice against the use of machinery. The prevailing opinion rather is, that throughout the whole process of the manufacture of a knife, the head and the hand must work together; and that to leave any part of the operation to machinery, would be only to mar it. American inventors and others have attempted to heap obloquy upon leading English cutlery firms because of their " slowness " in adopting machinery. It is only fair to such firms to say that, as far as they possibly can, they keep themselves thoroughly well posted up in all the improvements that are introduced in the shape of machinery; but up to the present time, they have seen no goods produced by it, that will bear comparison with those made by hand. This statement is fully confirmed by the fact that, for all the better descriptions of goods, and particularly carvers, the Americans cannot touch us, though in the manufacture of the cheaper articles they are competing successfully with us, and will in all probability eventually control their own market.

Trade marks have played an important part in the history of cutlery and are found upon the most ancient and rudest specimens that have been preserved to us. Prior to, and during the earlier years of the reign of Elizabeth, they appear to have been assigned to the different manufacturers by a court leet and a certain number of cutlers sitting as a jury. As reading was by no means a general accomplishment, it was not usual to stamp goods with their maker's name, but to use a bull's head or some other sign which the people could readily understand. Even in those days, the mark of a manufacturer whose goods had attained to celebrity, was frequently pirated, and that led, in 1624, to the incorporation of the Cutlers' Company of Hallamshire. To them was given the power to assign trade marks, and also to search any dwelling house in which there was reason to believe that goods bearing a fictitious mark were concealed. Any manufacturer whose mark was infringed within a radius of six miles round Sheffield, could obtain summary redress before the magistrates, but for any infringement outside of that boundary, he was left to the ordinary laws of the realm, and had to establish his right to the mark by use and not by grant. Even with this protection, the trade mark of Messrs. Rodgers and other eminent firms was continually being pirated, and it was seen to be absolutely necessary that the law should be made more stringent, and at the instance mainly of the Sheffield Chamber of Commerce, the Legislature were induced to pass the Trades Marks Act of 1862. That Act operated as a very wholesome terror to wrong-doers, and in a very short time the practice of infringing trade marks was almost, if not altogether, put an end to. English manufacturers have had another and still greater difficulty to contend with. For a long time it was the practice of German manufacturers to stamp the name and mark of some well-known English house upon goods of a very inferior character, send them to London, and transship them without allowing them to land, thereby preventing the Custom House officers from examining them. The goods were sent abroad, and advertised as the manufacture of the firms whose mark they bore. The Chambers of Commerce, after considerable trouble, succeeded in prevailing upon the Legislature to amend the Customs Act, so as to enable officers to seize and detain goods in transit, as well as goods imported inwards. It was also well known that German manufacturers were willing to supply English houses with goods bearing their own corporate mark, at such prices as rendered it almost impossible for an honest English tradesman to compete with them. This dishonourable practice has also been put a stop to by a further amendment of the Customs Act, which now renders liable to seizure any foreign goods whatever bearing an English name or the name of a place in England. Every mark that is granted is registered, and its owner has its exclusive use preserved to him by laws of a most stringent character, advantages which to a fair dealing honest manufacturer are of great importance, and of almost more than money value.

It may seem almost paradoxical, but this same system of trades' marks, incalculable an advantage as it is on the one hand, is on the other hand the greatest bane known to the cutlery trade, and the manufacturers appear altogether unable to relieve themselves from it. The evil is by no means of recent growth, but modern times have seen it very largely extended. From time immemorial it has been the practice for Sheffield firms to stamp upon some of the goods they made, the names of their customers, who of course have retailed them as their own productions. This has been felt by the manufacturers to be a great hardship, as it has prevented them from becoming known, and others have won the honours to which they were entitled. Many years ago Messrs. Rodgers decided to strike a blow at this system, knowing full well the penalty which they would have to pay. It happened in this way. A son of one of the members of the firm went into a shop in London, and asked for a knife marked " Rodgers and Sons." He was shown one, and when he asked if it could be warranted, the tradesman produced a knife made by the same firm but bearing his own name, and said that one he could warrant. The firm thereupon decided to stamp henceforth no other name than their own. They have since abided by their determination, although at the expense of being almost entirely excluded from the London and other home markets. At the time several firms supported them in their efforts to remove this grievance, but they had eventually to yield, and now there are not probably more than a dozen firms who strike exclusively their own mark. Indeed competition in the trade is now so keen, that any customer doing the smallest possible retail business, can have his name stamped on the goods he may order, however trifling they may be in value. The practice in many ways seriously interferes with the proper conduct of business. A manufacturer can do little in the way of working a stock, as he is not certain of the continuance of the favours of his customers. He is further placed at a disadvantage by having to execute each order, however small, separately, and when the goods are left upon his hands, as is not unfrequently the case, he has to dispose of them at a loss, or, as is possible with some goods, grind out the mark and restamp them. Unionism has taken deep root among the men, and the employers have from time to time felt its power and influence, but they have made little or no attempt to combine amongst themselves. Had they done so, they could have relieved themselves from this, as well as some other evils which afflict the trade.

One great drawback to the prosperity of the cutlery trade, is that very little capital is required to embark in it. Numbers of the men, dissatisfied with their earnings, commence business on their own account, and become what is popularly termed "little masters," though the change can scarcely be said to have improved their position. They have to pay dearly for the inferior material which they purchase; they put into it as a rule their own labour, and the goods when completed represent all their capital. They must sell them; a fact of which the factor or merchant who buys for the London, Liverpool, Manchester, and other leading markets, is well aware. He is able to name his own terms, and they are such as to leave the producer little margin of profit and very frequently nothing for his own labour. The evil unfortunately is not confined to himself, but interferes most injuriously with the respectable maker in the conduct of his business. He has not only to remunerate all the labour which he engages, but to live himself, and his goods when placed side by side with those of the "little master" appear expensive, when in reality they are not so. The difference to the eye of the uninitiated may not be great; but as regards quality and workmanship, the one will not bear the slightest comparison with the other. The number of what might be termed "leading firms" in the trade is only small. Such firms, for instance, as Messrs. Rodgers, have in their employ, in addition to clerks, warehouse people, and others, about 1200 skilled workmen, who turn out weekly 5000 dozens of table knives and forks, 1500 pairs of carvers, 1500 dozens of pocket-knives, 1200 dozens of razors, and 1200 dozens of scissors.

As the trade has progressed to such a marvellous extent, it might have been expected that the working cutler would have improved with it, but such is not the case. There is very little if any change to be seen in him, and taking the trade throughout, his position is by no means an enviable one. He is to-day almost as uncultivated in his manners and vulgar in his tastes, and as improvident in his habits, as at any time during the last fifty years. Of course there are noble exceptions of men who have read and thought, and by persevering industry have improved their positions in life; but unfortunately they are not numerous. The reasons for this are not far to seek. The trade is divided into a multitude of branches, and a man taking to one of them has the same dull round of duty to perform from one year's end to another. His work may, and doubtless does, require the greatest skill and the closest attention; and the slightest slip might mar the work of hours, but after all, it is working at the same thing over and over again, until his mind becomes dwarfed and stunted, and he has neither the energy nor the desire to strike out new paths for himself or to distinguish himself in his trade. There is an old proverb, "as poor as a cutler," and it is as true to-day as ever it was. The men have been striving for years to obtain better wages; and have from time to time succeeded in getting slight advances, though not at all in comparison with the increased cost of living. The wages of skilled workmen in the employ of the best and largest houses only average 30s. per week, and there can be no doubt that those of the inferior workmen who are engaged by the "little masters" are very much less, and they are poor indeed. The great bulk of the men are exceedingly improvident and neglect their homes for the public-house. They take their wives generally from amongst the girls employed in the warehouses; and as they are not domesticated, they make no attempt to render their homes attractive. Then there is no class of artisans, in Sheffield at least, amongst whom the vice of gambling has spread with a more demoralizing effect than amongst the cutlers.

In some of the large manufactories 90 per cent. of the workmen employed are addicted to the habit, and frequently their week's wages are pawned before half of them are earned. The employers are fully aware of the existence of the evil, and see the results of it both in the men and in their work; but they are altogether powerless to check it. The men have also been seriously affected by the operations of the Factory and Education Acts. They had been accustomed to avail themselves extensively of child labour; but the Acts have happily put an end to that system, to the very great advantage, it is hoped, of the next generation of cutlers. Very much might be done by way of improving the social condition of the men, if the Government and the public generally would purchase more freely of the better classes of goods, and not the cheapest and most worthless. The trade would then fall into the hands of well-known respectable firms, who would be able to pay better wages, as they would not have the "little master" with his inferior goods underselling them.

The principal markets for English cutlery are America, Canada, Havana, Australia, New Zealand, India, South America, and the Cape. Fine goods are, to a limited extent, sent to Russia, Belgium, Persia, and Turkey; and the cheaper class to China, Burmah, Japan, and Cabool. In some of these markets French and German manufactures are competing successfully with English houses, particularly in the common descriptions of goods. As regards the better class of articles, our own manufacturers are yet able fully to hold their own against the world, and will no doubt continue to do so, as long as the high character which their goods have acquired is maintained. The trade is even now passing through a period of considerable development, but at the same time of great depression, and to what higher stages in design and workmanship it may reach when it shall again revive, it would be impossible to predict.